It's the End Of the World

As we know it

It's The End Of The World As we know it

Richard
Bradbury

PNEUMA SPRINGS PUBLISHING UK

Unless otherwise indicated, Scripture quotations are taken from the New American Standard Bible, version of the Holy Bible.

First Published 2006

Published by Pneuma Springs Publishing

It's the End of the World as we know it

ISBN10: 0-9545510-6-0

ISBN13: 978-0-954551-06-3

Cover design, editing and typesetting by:
Pneuma Springs Publishing
A Subsidiary of Pneuma Springs Ltd.
230 Lower Road, Belvedere Kent, DA17 6DE.
E: admin@pneumasprings.co.uk
W: www.pneumasprings.co.uk

A catalogue record for this book is available from the British Library.

Dedication

This book is dedicated to my wife and family who have supported and encouraged me throughout this journey.

Also, to my father whose teaching has been foundational in my life.

Finally, to Stuart and Irene for their inspirational leadership of the Groundlevel network.

TABLE OF CONTENTS

INTRODUCTION

There have been many words written and books produced concerning the End Times. Differing and conflicting theories abound and each writer approaches this subject from the prejudice of their own doctrinal predisposition.

My aim in this book is to present and consider each of the most common theories propounded on its merits, in order to give the reader an opportunity to make up his or her own mind as to which theory or combination of theories is the correct one.

In the end, there is only one theory which will be proved accurate and that is God's. In the mean time, we are left with the challenge of trying to pick out from the prophetic and apocalyptic literature contained within the Bible a theory which best fits all the scriptures. To say the least, this is testing, hence the reason why there has been so much debate and discussion (and error) concerning this subject over the years.

Why is it important to have a coherent eschatological[1] view? Shouldn't, we concentrate on the issues we face in our world today and let the future take care of itself? This is certainly one position commonly held by Christians of all persuasions. However, as will become clear in this book, our understanding of the End Times does affect the way we view and approach the issues facing us as individuals, churches, denominations and as the Universal Church[2].

Whilst we wait for the End Times to unfold, this book is an attempt to pull together the various theories into one, easy to understand, guide in order to enable the reader to navigate their own course through these dangerous and turbulent waters.

A common approach to this subject is to start from the book of Revelation and then to build an eschatological position from the visions contained within it. This approach is criticised by certain theologians who suggest that, since Revelation is, by its very nature, symbolic, any literal interpretation of the events contained therein is flawed, especially some of the events recorded in Revelation 19 onwards[3]. A safer

[1] *Eschatology is the branch of theology concerned with the end of the world from the Greek word Eskhatos meaning last.*

[2] *The 'Universal Church' is a theological term used to refer to people of all denominations who hold the Christian faith anywhere in the world at a given point in time.*

[3] *An example is the millennial reign of Christ which is a pillar of much eschatology (theories are nominated as being 'post-millennial', 'pre-millennial' 'or 'a-millennial'), however, the only place the Millennium is explicitly mentioned in the whole of the Bible is in Revelation 20:2, 4 & 7.*

approach is to see Revelation as the summation of apocalyptic vision and to allow the rest of the Bible (especially those passages where clear teaching is given such as Matthew 24 & 25 and 1 Thessalonians 4 and 2 Thessalonians) to interpret these events for us. This is the approach I will be taking throughout this book.

Of key importance to understanding the End Times is to consider the future of Israel. Some would argue that Israel has no specific future in the purposes of God and that the nation forewent their privileged position as 'God's chosen people' when they rejected the Messiah. They further argue that the Church is now the recipient of all the promises which God gave to Israel and is in effect 'the new Israel'. Others would argue that the Church is an interim measure until God gets his purposes for Israel back on track. We will consider the Israel debate in the opening chapter of this book since the position we take concerning Israel will influence the view we take concerning the consummation of the Kingdom at the return of Christ. From here we will examine the most common theories concerning the End Times in order to provide a framework in which we can consider the apocalyptic and prophetic literature of the Old and New Testaments.

The first part of this book, then, is a consideration of the various theories which abound concerning the End Times and the latter part is a detailed study of the various prophetic scriptures in both the Old and the New Testaments, beginning with the book of Daniel.

As we begin in Daniel, our studies will commence, not with the future, but with historical events. At first sight it might appear to be an odd approach to go backwards in order to go forwards. However, Daniel lived at a time when the life he had known had been demolished, with the destruction of Jerusalem and the captivity of the people of Israel away from the Land which Moses, under God's command, had led them to possess. It is perhaps not surprising therefore, that in the midst of such turbulent times he should receive visions of future turbulence, especially as it would affect the people of Israel.

As we begin to study the revelations given to Daniel it will become clear that these visions were not just given for his own time but actually cover the whole sweep of human history through to the return of Christ. Whilst other prophets prior to Daniel had received prophecies which concerned the End Times (see, for example, Isaiah 65:17-25), it is in

Daniel that we first encounter the prophetic visions placed within the context of actual human history. Thus, Daniel provides us with a framework into which we can place all other scriptures concerning the End Times.

Some may disagree with this approach. Daniel has been much maligned by certain theologians over the years on the basis of the fact (as we shall see) that the prophecies contained within it, so accurately reflect the events as they unfolded in the centuries subsequent to Daniel's time. It is suggested, on this basis, that the book of Daniel must have been written much later. However, this approach assumes that the receipt of such Divine revelation is not feasible, reasonable or rational. Contrary to this, our starting point in this study is the acceptance that God is real and that at various times in history, he has chosen to reveal his plans and purposes to his servants the prophets (Amos 3:7).

After Daniel, we will review the remaining Old Testament books which make reference to the End Times. We will then turn our attention to the Book of Revelation. From there, we will examine the clear teaching of the New Testament concerning the End Times. Inevitably, in this process, some reference will be made back to both the Old Testament and to the book of Revelation.

Finally, in section 4, we will conclude this study by examining some of the post-End Times events.

Before we commence our study it is sensible to introduce some of the events and characters of the End Times. These events will be referred to throughout this book as we examine this subject and therefore a clear understanding of these things is essential to understanding the whole period known as the End Times.

No attempt will be made here to position these events or to argue for their literal or symbolical occurrence or otherwise. Such positioning will be suggested in subsequent chapters. The purpose here is merely to give a definition of these items.

The Tribulation

The tribulation is a period of time in the years just prior to the Second Coming of Christ, during which great hardship will be experienced on the earth. Daniel refers to this period as a time of 'great distress' (Daniel

12:1). Jesus said that it will be a time of 'great tribulation such as has not occurred since the beginning of the world' (Matthew 24:21).

It is understood that the book of Revelation is largely a description of some of the key events of this period because it will be a time in which judgement will be unleashed on the earth in the form of wars, natural cataclysmic events, plagues, famine and persecution.

Again it is understood (as will become clear in this study) that this period will last for seven years (whether this is seven literal years or a short period of time is a matter of interpretation) and will culminate in the return of Christ to the earth. Jesus also said of this period that 'unless those days had been cut short, no life would have been saved' (Matthew 24:22).

The Unholy Trinity

The Unholy Trinity appear together in the Book of Revelation, chapters 12 to 13. Essentially, they comprise Satan, the Antichrist and the False Prophet.

These three play a significant role in the Tribulation and will be dealt with summarily on the return of Christ to the earth.

The Rapture

The rapture is an event which has been debated in the Church for many years. Essentially, it is the supernatural removal of the Church (genuine believers in Christ Jesus) from the world and the translation of the same into a new, eternal state of being.

This event includes both the living and the dead at His coming. Much of the debate concerning the rapture has been around when this event will actually occur, and, for some, whether it will occur at all. These differing viewpoints will be discussed in chapter 3.

The Resurrection

During the period of the End Times, the dead will be brought back to life. Revelation 20 verse 5 implies that there are multiple resurrections. Again, this may be seen as being problematic since these passages in Revelation are largely symbolic. We will return to this subject later on in this study but, suffice to say, the righteous dead will be raised to life and the unrighteous dead will be raised to judgement.

The Second Coming

The Second Coming is the physical return of Christ to the earth. Some would argue that this is a two-part event with Christ coming once for the Church and once in judgement. Again, the various viewpoints on this will be discussed in chapter 4.

What is clear from the Bible is that there was an expectation in the minds of the apostles that Jesus would return. John concludes the book of Revelation with the following words, spoken by Jesus himself: 'Yes I am coming quickly'. To this John adds 'Amen. Come Lord Jesus'.

The Millennium

The Millennium is a period of time during which Christ will reign over the earth. Obviously, it is anticipated that this will be for one thousand years; however, some would argue that the term 'millennium' is representative of a significant period of time and therefore does not imply a literal thousand years.

Others would argue that since Christ already reigns supreme over heaven and earth, we are already in the Millennium, and that this period will be concluded at His return.

Still others would suggest that since the only place that a period of a thousand years is referred to is in Revelation 20, and that since Revelation is largely a symbolic book, there is no certainty that the Millennium will occur at all as a literal event.

All of these viewpoints will be discussed and considered in chapter 3.

The Judgements

In Revelation 20, the period of the End Times concludes with a number of judgements, including the judgement of Satan, and the judgement of the unsaved. The End Time judgements will be discussed in Chapter 15, however, suffice to say for the moment that a time of judgement or reckoning is coming for all those who have inhabited the earth from beginning to end.

The Judgement of the Nations

Many Old Testament scriptures speak of a time of judgement upon the nations. This is perceived as being concurrent with the return of Christ, when the nations will be gathered for war against Israel / Jerusalem, and the Messiah will return to rescue the nation and to mete out the final judgement upon the nations of the world.

The Restoration of Israel

Once again, many Old Testament scriptures speak of the physical restoration of the people of Israel to the land prior to the coming of the Messiah. This obviously took place historically following the exile, however, it is envisaged that Israel will again be gathered in the years leading up to the End Times and it could be that this began in 1947 with the re-establishment of the nationhood of Israel.

Armed with these brief definitions, let us begin our study.

Section 1

THE DOCTRINES OF THE END TIMES

Chapter 1

Israel and the Messianic Kingdom

Introduction

One important concern over which the Church has disagreed for centuries is the place of Israel in God's ongoing purposes, particularly as it affects the End Times. The position one takes on this important subject is fundamental to the eschatological view one adopts.

The reason for the lack of clarity concerning this subject is the apparent disconnect between the Old and New Testaments. If we read the Old Testament scriptures alone, no explicit reference is made to the Church and all the prophecy relates to Israel. Thus, when Jesus came and declared 'I will build my Church' (as opposed to Moses church), suddenly all of the prophetic scriptures needed to be reconsidered in the light of this new entity which entered the picture: the mystery of Christ (Ephesians 3:1-13). The problem is that if the Gentiles are 'fellow heirs and members of the body' (Ephesians 3:6), does God still have any purpose for those Jews who, according to their natural descent are children of Abraham and thereby heirs of promise, but who have rejected God's New Covenant in Christ and therefore are excluded from the 'new man' (Ephesians 2:15).

There are essentially three positions available to us concerning Israel's place in God's purposes:

1. Israel has no further role in the purposes of God. They forewent their role when they rejected the Messiah. God's purposes rest solely in the Church.
2. God's prime purposes rest with Israel and the Church is a temporary or interim measure until Israel returns to Him.
3. God has a separate agenda for Israel alongside his purposes for the Church and he will bring those two purposes together at the Return of Christ.

The first of these views has been by propagated by A-Millennialists[4] and Post-Millennialists, and was adopted by much of the Charismatic movement in its teaching on the Kingdom of God. The second of these views has been adopted by Pre-Millennialists as they have sought to fit the Bible around their Dispensational doctrines. The third view we will consider later on.

If we take the first position, all prophetic scriptures regarding the future of Israel have to be re-interpreted and spiritualised to be made relevant for the Church. This can prove tortuous in the extreme, particularly when we consider the volume of scriptures which speak of the restoration of the nation of Israel to the Land and the coming of the Messiah and the judgement of the nations. Following this line of interpretation, the land becomes the World, and Israel becomes the Church exclusively and most of the scriptures lose their historical and prophetic context.

On the other hand, taking the Pre-Millennial position, we run the danger of largely excluding the Church from the End Times which does not do justice to the very clear teaching given in the New Testament.

In this chapter, each of these views will be examined in more detail on its own merits to see if we can come to a conclusion as to what scripture itself teaches.

Covenants Concerning Israel

Our starting point for this study is to consider the various covenants

[4] *A- Millennialism, Pre-Millennialism, Post-Millennialism and Dispensationalism will be discussed in the Chapter 3.*

made with Israel, since each of these covenants contains promises which God has bound himself to keep.

The Abrahamic Covenant

In Genesis, God spoke to Abraham on a number of different occasions and each time he chose to reveal a little more of his purposes for Abraham and his descendents. The output from each of these occasions is summarised below:

Genesis 12:1-3 tells us:

- Abraham will be made a great nation.
- He will be blessed and his name will be made great.
- Those who bless him will be blessed; those who curse him will be cursed.
- In him all the families of the earth will be blessed.

Genesis 15:18-21 tells us:

- The land is given to Abraham's descendents, from 'the river of Egypt all the way to the Euphrates'.
- The people of the land are given into his hands.

In Genesis 17:1-8 God establishes a covenant of circumcision with Abraham. We are told that:

- He will be multiplied exceedingly
- He will be the father of a multitude of nations
- God will make nations and kings come out of Abraham
- This covenant will be *'an everlasting covenant'*
- God will give the land of Canaan to them as *'an everlasting possession'*

In Genesis 22:15 God gives further detail concerning this covenant:

- God will multiply his seed 'as the stars of the heavens and as the sand which is on the seashore'
- His seed will 'posses the gates of their enemies'

In Genesis 26:23-24, 28:13-15 and 35:9-12 the promises are confirmed to

Isaac and Jacob respectively.

The Mosaic Covenant

In Exodus 6:7-8 God confirmed to Moses, that he will be their (Israel's) God and that he will take them in to possess the land. He reaffirmed that this is to fulfil the promises of the covenant made with Abraham, Isaac and Jacob (v.8).

In Exodus 20 ff, the Law is given for obedience and for guidance of the people of Israel and the covenant is confirmed. Building upon this, in Deuteronomy 28:58-68 we see the consequences of disobedience: curses and disinheritance. In verses 63-65 Israel are told, '...you will be torn from the land where you are entering to possess it. Moreover, the Lord will scatter you among all peoples from one end of the earth to the other end of the earth.... Among those nations you will find no rest, and there will be no resting place for the sole of your foot.' This has typified the history of the Jewish people for three millennia.

In Deuteronomy 30:1-14 we see that, despite the promise of **dispersion** for disobedience, there is also a promise of **restoration** to the land for obedience. See particularly verses 3 to 5: 'Then the Lord your God will restore you from captivity and have compassion on you, and will gather you again from all the peoples where the Lord your God has scattered you. If your outcasts are at the ends of the earth, from there the Lord your God will bring you into the land which your fathers possessed, **and you shall possess it...'.**

The Davidic Covenant

In 2 Samuel 7:8-17 we see the covenant made by God with David. These verses tell us:

- God will establish a Kingdom with David's descendent as king.
- **This Kingdom will be established forever:** 'Your Kingdom shall endure before me forever; your throne shall be established forever'.

In Isaiah chapters 9 & 11 we see this covenant reconfirmed. Note particularly the following verses:

9:6-7 'For a child will be born to us, a son will be given to us; and the government will rest on His shoulders; and His name will be called Wonderful Counsellor, Mighty God, Eternal Father, Prince of Peace. There will be no end to the increase of His government or of peace, **on the throne of David and over his Kingdom, to establish it and to uphold it with justice and righteousness, from then on and forevermore.** The zeal of the Lord of hosts will accomplish this.'

Through this prophecy it is confirmed that the Davidic covenant will be confirmed through the Messiah - his coming will herald the commencement of the eternal reign of a descendent of David and the establishment of **an everlasting Kingdom.**

Principles Arising from the Covenants

Thus, essentially we can identify seven principles which arise from these various covenants with Israel:

1. There is an everlasting covenant with the seed of Abraham.
2. The land of Israel is an everlasting possession for Israel.
3. If they are obedient, they will be blessed and will possess the land.
4. If they are disobedient they will be dispossessed and scattered.
5. If they repent they will be restored to the land and will possess it once more.
6. God will establish a king on David's throne forever.
7. This king will be a descendent of David.

The promises to Israel are **everlasting** (cf. Isaiah 54:10, Jeremiah 33:25-26). Our view of the End Times must take account of these principles; however, we also need to review them in the light of the New Covenant.

The New Covenant

The starting point of the New Covenant is the recognition that Jesus is the Messiah. He is the descendent of David who came to establish the everlasting Kingdom. From the commencement of his ministry (Matthew 4:17 & 23, Mark 1:14) he proclaimed that the Kingdom had come. Clearly, from the teaching of Jesus, as laid out in the gospels, there was more to this Kingdom than a portion of land in the Middle East.

However, even Jesus' disciples had problems grasping this concept. In Acts 1:1-8 we see them still reducing the Kingdom down to dominion over the land of Israel ('is it at this time you are restoring the Kingdom to Israel' (1:6)). They had an understanding that he was indeed the Messiah, but did not at this time fully understand what this meant in terms of the realm over which Jesus' Kingdom stretched. Jesus, in response to this question, told them in effect to mind their own business about the political Kingdom of Israel but to make sure that they are baptised in the Spirit in order to be his witnesses to the ends of the earth.

Soon after this, Jesus ascended into heaven to be seated at the right hand of the Father in Heaven (Acts 2:33-36), 'waiting from that time onward until His enemies be made a footstool for his feet' (Hebrews 10:13, Psalm 110:1). Thus, the time between Jesus' ascension and his second coming is the time in which his Kingdom on earth is his reign in and through the lives of all those who submit to his lordship[5]. It is not a political reign but a spiritual reign[6] which extends beyond the borders of Israel to include the whole world.

In Acts chapters 10 and 11, we see the Good News of the Kingdom opened up to the Gentiles in addition to the Jews and the half-breed Samaritans. This is a seminal moment in the development of the Kingdom. If non-Jews are included in this Kingdom, it cannot possibly be restricted to the political Kingdom of Israel. From this point on in Acts, Paul becomes the champion of the Gentile church, spreading the gospel throughout the Greek speaking world. It is from Paul's teachings that the concept of the world-wide spiritual Kingdom is developed. We find that:

- Entrance into this Kingdom is not on the basis of lineage but through **Justification** (Romans 1-4) and is no longer on the basis of birth or of fulfilling the Mosaic Law; instead it is on the basis of **Faith** in the completed work of Christ alone.
- Paul makes it clear that God is not working out his purposes through two peoples but through one people:

For He himself is our peace who made both groups into one and broke

5 *Some would argue that, since Jesus is reigning, we are now in the Millennium. For a consideration of this view see Chapters 2 & 3.*

6 *AAlthough at times the Church has taken on a political dimension, for example, during the Middle Ages through the papacy. However, it is clear from scripture that Jesus was not interested in political power but spiritual regeneration which would impact the social and political world.*

down the barrier of the dividing wall, by abolishing in His flesh enmity, which is the Law of commandments contained in ordinances, so that in Himself He might make the two into one new man, thus establishing peace, and might reconcile them both in one body to God through the cross, by it having put to death the enmity… You are fellow citizens with the saints and are of God's household. (Ephesians 2:14-22).

…You being a wild olive were grafted in among them and became a partaker of the rich root of the olive tree… (Romans 11:17).

In other words, the Church is not created as a new and separate people from the Jews, but we have been reconciled with them in God's purposes so that, in Christ Jesus, we can enjoy 'every spiritual blessing in the heavenly places'. We are not partakers in the physical blessings of Israel (the land, etc.) but we are partakers in the spiritual blessings of the covenants made with Israel: '…it is those who are of faith who are sons of Abraham…'

- Peter, in 1 Peter 2:9, talking to the church (both Jew and Gentile) says,

But you are a chosen race, a royal priesthood, a holy nation, a people for God's own possession, so that you may proclaim the excellencies of him who called you out of darkness into his marvellous light; for once you were not a people, but now you are the people of God; you had not received mercy, but now you have received mercy.

Clearly, the language previously attributed exclusively to Israel is now being used of God's New Covenant people (c.f. Exodus 19:5-6 and Hebrews 12:18-29).

This raises three questions:

1. If we are justified by faith where does this leave those still under the Law?
2. If we are now the People of God, where does this leave the Jews who are descended from Abraham but have rejected Jesus as the Messiah?
3. Are the promises to Abraham, Isaac, Jacob, Moses and David concerning the Jews still valid?

In seeking to answer these questions we will consider two postulations which have been taught by various people and at various times throughout Church history, Replacement Theology and Dispensational Theology, and then we will consider a third position which, perhaps, gives us a more consistent framework within which to view the End Times.

Replacement Theology

Replacement theology teaches that the Church has replaced Israel in the purposes of God. It teaches that all of God's purposes and all the blessings promised in the Old Testament find their fulfilment in the Church. In so doing, it suggests that God no longer has any purpose for Israel and that they are like any other nation: simply a people to be evangelised.

Many Charismatic churches have propagated this doctrine. Unfortunately, as we will discover, it does not accord with scripture. A fairly cursory look at Romans 11 will confirm this, for example Romans 11:25-26 says, 'All Israel will be saved', clearly indicating that God still has a purpose for the people of Israel. In addition, in order for Replacement Theology to be adopted, all of the covenantal promises to Israel examined above have to be taken as non-literal for them to be fulfilled in the Church. For example, in order to deal with promises concerning Israel inheriting the land 'forever', we have to spiritualise our understanding of both Israel and the land so that the land becomes the World (or Heaven) and Israel becomes the Church.

The problem with this kind of interpretation is that it is inconsistent, for example, we can take the prophecies of Jeremiah (Jeremiah 29:10) concerning the restoration of Israel literally, but any prophecies concerning the end time restoration of Israel under this interpretation are for the Church only. This does not make logical or hermeneutical sense, especially when you consider passages such as Isaiah 9:6-7 where the first and second coming of Christ are included in the same passage; in such cases you have to interpret the first part for Israel ('for unto us a child is born') and the second part for the Church ('of the increase of His government and peace there will be no end on the throne of David and over his Kingdom').

Replacement Theology is thus inconsistent, illogical and does not accord with the explicit teaching of scripture such as we find in Romans chapters 9 to 11.

Dispensational Theology

There was no theology of Dispensationalism before John Nelson Darby (founder of the exclusive Brethren) and Charles Russell (founder of the Jehovah's Witnesses). Dispensational theology was made popular through the Schofield Bible which included Schofield's notes, which were written from a dispensational predisposition. This theology was later adopted by the Pentecostal Movement and became the standard interpretation of the End Times up until the rise of the Charismatic Movement, which generally adopted a Post-Millennial, Replacement theological position.

Dispensationalists divide up the whole of history into 7 dispensations[7]. These are defined as follows:

- 1st Dispensation: **Innocence** – Man was created innocent, set up in an ideal environment, placed under a simple test and warned of the result of disobedience. The woman fell through pride; the man deliberately (1 Timothy 2:14). Although God restored the sinning creatures, the dispensation came to an end at the judgement and expulsion from Eden.

- 2nd Dispensation: **Conscience** – Adam to Noah. By an act of disobedience man comes to an experiential knowledge of good and evil. Driven out of Eden and placed under the Adamic Covenant (Genesis 3:17-19), man was accountable to do all known good and to abstain from all known evil and to come before God by sacrifice. The result of this testing was complete degeneration ending in the judgement of the flood.

- 3rd Dispensation: **Human Government** - Noah to Abraham. The declaration of the Noahic Covenant after the flood (Genesis 8:20-9:27) put man under a new test, featured by the inauguration of human government, the highest function of which is the judicial

[7] *A dispensation is an era of time during which man is tested in respect to obedience to some definite revelation of God's will.*

taking of life. Man is responsible to govern the world for God. That responsibility rests upon the whole race, Jews & Gentiles. With the failure of Israel under the Palestinian Covenant (Deut 28:30) and the consequent judgement of the captives "the Times of the Gentiles" (Luke 21:24) began. The world is still Gentile-governed, and hence this dispensation overlaps other dispensations, and will not strictly come to an end until the second coming of Christ.

- 4th Dispensation: **Promise** – Abraham to Moses. From the call of Abraham (Genesis 12:1) to the giving of the Mosaic law (Exodus 19:8). This dispensation was under the Abrahamic Covenant and was exclusively Israelite.

- 5th Dispensation : **Law** – Moses to Christ. This era reaches from Sinai to Calvary. The period was a school master to bring Israel to Christ and was governed by the Mosaic Covenant (Exodus 20:1-31:18).

- 6th Dispensation: **Grace** – Christ to just before the Tribulation. This period began with the death and resurrection of Christ (Romans 3:24-26; 4:24 & 25). The point of testing is no longer legal obedience to the Law as a condition of salvation, but acceptance or rejection of Christ with good works as a fruit of salvation (John 1:12, 3:36, 1 John 5:10-12). The predicted end of the testing of man under grace is the apostasy of the professing church (2 Timothy 3:1-8) and the subsequent apocalyptic judgements.

- 7th Dispensation – **The Kingdom**. This is the last of the ordered ages regulating human life on the earth, previous to the eternal state. It involves the establishment of the Kingdom covenanted to David (2 Samuel 7:8-17, Zechariah 12:8, Luke 1:32-33; Luke 12:8). This will include Israel's restoration and conversion (Romans 11:25-27) and her rehabilitation as a high-priestly nation in fellowship with God and as head over the Millennial nations (Zechariah 3:1-10, 6:9-15).

This summarises Dispensationalism, however, there are a number of problems with this theology as just described:

- It sees the covenant of grace as just a period in history during which man is being tested in a different way, instead of it being THE means of salvation and THE final word from God (Hebrews 1:1-2, 10:11-12). Jesus is the fulfilment of all that has gone before. 'The gospel ... is THE power of God for salvation to everyone who believes to the Jew first and also to the Greek'. There is no new word of salvation coming. All God's dealings past present and future, whether with Adam, Noah, Abraham, Moses, David or us, are on the basis of grace working through faith (see Romans chapter 4) not on the basis of dispensations.

- It puts off the Kingdom to the Millennium. This is contrary to the teaching of Jesus and neither was it the understanding of the New Testament writers. A cursory look at the gospels and Jesus' emphasis on the Kingdom show this position to be an untenable one unless you ignore Jesus' teaching on the Kingdom - something you do at your own risk[8].

[8] *Dispensationalists propound 'The Postponement Theory' in which they say that John and Jesus proclaimed that the Kingdom, that is, the Jewish theocracy, was at hand. But because the Jews did not repent and believe, Jesus postponed its establishment until His Second Coming. The pivotal point marking the change is placed by Schofield in Matthew 11:20 and by others in Matthew 12. Before that turning point Jesus did not concern himself with the Gentiles but preached the Gospel of the Kingdom to Israel; and after that he did not preach the Kingdom anymore, but only predicted its future coming and offered rest to the weary of both Israel and the Gentiles. But it cannot be maintained that Jesus did not concern Himself with the Gentiles before the supposed turning point (cf. Matthew 8:5-13; John 4:1-42), nor that after it He ceased to preach the Kingdom (Matthew 13, Luke 10:1-11). There is absolutely no proof that Jesus preached two different gospels, first the gospel of the Kingdom and then the gospel of the grace of God; in the light of scripture, this distinction is untenable. Jesus never had in mind the re-establishment of the Old Testament Theocracy, but the introduction of the spiritual reality of which the Old Testament Kingdom was but a type (Matthew 8:11,12, 13:31-33, 21:43, Luke 17:21, John 3:3, 18:36-37, cf. Romans 14:17). He did not postpone the task for which he had come into the world, but actually established the Kingdom and referred to it more than once as a present reality (Matthew 11:12, 12:28, Luke 17:21, John 18:36-37, cf. Colossians 1:13). This whole postponement theory is a comparatively recent fiction, and is very objectionable, because it breaks up the unity of scripture and of the people of God in an unwarranted way.....Besides, we get two peoples of God, the one natural and the other spiritual, the one earthly and the other heavenly, as if Jesus did not speak of 'one flock and one shepherd' (John 10:16), and as if Paul did not say that the Gentiles were grafted into the old olive tree (Romans 11:17).*

Quotation taken from Louis Berkhof's Systematic Theology p.714.

- In order to fit scripture into its doctrine it has to get rid of the Church prior to the Tribulation (see Chapter 3). This contradicts explicit scriptural passages concerning the rapture, such as Matthew 24:29-31, and is based on inference. The argument can only be sustained by predisposing that Israel only are left during the Tribulation and by therefore assuming that 'the elect' are Israel only, which contradicts Paul's use of the word in Romans 8:33.

- Dispensationalists teach that the covenant with Abraham has been superseded. However, according to Galatians 3:29, we are heirs according to the promise, and the Covenant with Abraham still stands – it has not been superseded and God still deals with us on the same basis: Faith and Promise.

- Dispensationalism teaches that the Church is God's 'Plan B' because of Israel's failure. When Israel is restored, the Church will become fairly irrelevant. This also assumes that Jesus failed in His first purpose of coming to earth and had to run with a substitute plan called 'The Church' (cf. Ephesians 1:18-23). Such a suggestion is close to heresy in attributing failure to the unerring God.

- Under Dispensationalism, the Church is excluded from the Millennial Kingdom since that is seen as belonging to Israel only. Instead the Church remains in Heaven until after the Millennium when it comes back into the picture as part of the New Heavens and the New Earth. However, Revelation 4:9-10 clearly states that the Church will reign on earth, and 1 Thessalonians 3:13 clearly states that Jesus will return 'with all His saints'. Some argue around this that the Church will indeed be present on earth during the Millennium but it is not exactly clear what they suppose the church will be doing.

A third position

Let us now consider a third theological position. The basic assumption of this position is that God is working out His purposes with Israel who are physically His chosen people, and that He is working out His purposes in parallel spiritually through the Church (Messianic Jews &

Gentiles brought together through Christ). On the return of Christ, the two purposes will be reunited under the Lordship of Christ who is Man of very Man and God of very God.

There are a number of principles which, if applied correctly, support this approach:

- A fundamental biblical hermeneutic is: first the physical, then the spiritual (type and anti-type). God illustrates a spiritual truth by physical type before fulfilling the spiritual reality. The book of Hebrews demonstrates in great detail the fact that the Tabernacle was a type which is fulfilled spiritually in Christ when he took his own blood into the Holy of Holies in Heaven and made a way for us to follow him. In 1 Corinthians 10:11, Paul tells us that the events which occurred to the People of Israel in the wilderness 'happened to them as an example, and they were written for our instruction on whom the ends of the ages have come.' In other words, God's dealings with Israel physically are a picture to us spiritually. What has been and will be fulfilled in them physically will be fulfilled in the Church spiritually.

- The literal promises of God to Abraham, Moses and David will be literally fulfilled. If God has said a king will sit on David's throne forever we cannot spiritualise it and say, 'what God meant was…' Christ will sit physically on the throne of Israel. God has given the land to Israel as an eternal possession. God's covenant with Abraham's seed will last forever.

- The promises given to Abraham, Isaac, Jacob, Moses and David will also spiritually come upon us who are children through the New Covenant (See Galatians 3 and Romans 9-11 for a discussion on this – we are grafted into the vine).

- The whole thrust of Ephesians is that all things will one day be united in Christ. That is the purpose which God is working out through the ages – to sum up all things in Christ (Ephesians 1:10); to break down the dividing wall and to make the two one (Ephesians 2:14).

When Christ returns, his physical promises to Israel and his spiritual promises which have come to the Church (which is made up of Jews and Gentiles who have been grafted into Israel) will all be fulfilled as he unites the Kingdom of Heaven and the kingdoms of the earth under His rulership. The nation of Israel will 'look on me whom they have pierced' (Zechariah 12:10) and will turn en masse to God, accepting Jesus both as the Messiah who died for them and whose blood has cleansed them from their sin, and as their Messianic King.

Jesus will rule physically on earth in Jerusalem, on David's throne, but he will not just rule the Kingdoms of this world but the Kingdom of Heaven too, simultaneously (Revelation 11:15, 1 Corinthians 15:24-25).

The New Jerusalem (Revelation 20) is made up of all saints throughout the ages who are His, both from Israel and from the Church. All things will be united under the headship of Jesus Christ.

The benefit of this approach is that Old Testament promises can be spiritualised without dismissing the literal fulfilment in Israel.

Summary

What does all this tell us in relation to our questions? Replacement Theology sees Israel as largely irrelevant to God's purposes; Dispensational Theology sees the Church as largely irrelevant to God's purposes; the third option is a marrying of the purposes of God for Israel and the Church. We can sum up as follows:

- The only means of coming to God is through Christ. Jews today, no matter how God-fearing, are outside of the New Covenant and therefore do not have access to God. Access is only possible through Christ.
- The Jews are still the Chosen People in that God's covenant with Abraham has not been rescinded. However, the Church is also the chosen people of God (1 Peter 2:9).
- The physical promises of the covenant concerning the Land, etc. are still in effect and will be physically fulfilled on earth. God's promise to restore Israel to the land has begun to be fulfilled in the years since 1947.
- From Romans 11 we find that, ultimately, Israel will turn en

masse to God when they 'look upon (him) whom they pierced' (Zechariah 12:10). At that time they will become the beneficiaries of the physical and spiritual promises of all the covenants.

If we take this alternative approach, as outlined above, we can say that we will share with them, having come into the commonwealth of Israel through acceptance of Christ.

Conclusion

The reader may choose to take up any of the above positions or a combination of these positions, however, what is clear is that without a clear view on the future of Israel, we cannot meaningfully approach the subject of the End Times, nor can we intelligently consider the prophetic and apocalyptic scriptures.

Chapter 2

The Role of the Church in the End Times

Introduction

The role we attribute to the church in the End Times is very much dependent on the theological framework we adopt as individuals and which we use to interpret the Bible. This is developed further in the next chapter; however, the purpose of this chapter is to examine the two main possibilities which have been postulated during church history regarding what happens to the church during the End Times, and specifically, during the period known as the Great Tribulation.

Is the Church involved at all at the Return of Christ?

Looking first at the position taken by Dispensational theology, in this eschatology the Church is raptured[9] prior to the commencement of the Tribulation and in fact this event signals its commencement. In other

[9] The rapture is discussed in more detail in Chapter 3. Suffice to say that the rapture is the removal from the earth of all believers, referred to in a number of places throughout the New Testament. The area of dispute concerning the rapture is whether it occurs prior to the tribulation or after it, and whether it is a physical or metaphorical event.

words, at a certain point in history, currently known only to the Father, the Church will be removed from the World en-masse and will be absent throughout the whole of the following seven years of the Tribulation and, in fact, through the Millennium.

The consequences of adopting this position on our view of the End Times are numerous, however, the following are two key issues:

1. A view on where the Church goes during the Tribulation has to be formed.
2. A view on the effect of the removal of the Church on the remaining world population during the Tribulation also needs to be developed.

Dispensationalists suggest that during the period of the Tribulation, the Church is in heaven enjoying the Marriage Supper of the Lamb (see Revelation 19:6-9). Furthermore, following the Tribulation, the Church either remains in heaven until after the Millennium and only comes back onto the scene of history after the new heavens and the new earth have been created, or comes back with Christ to reign in some form, although this is not usually developed by dispensationalists.

For Dispensationalists, the time prior to the Tribulation is a time of great apostasy and falling away so that by the time Jesus comes to remove the Church at the Rapture, it is only the faithful few who are left. Scriptures cited to support this include Matthew 24:12, 1 Timothy 4:1 and 2 Thessalonians 2:3.

Of particular importance to Dispensationalists is the notion that the seven churches to which Christ writes at the start of Revelation represent seven successive periods in Church history. This development ends with the apostate Church, exemplified in the letter to the Laodiceans who are described as being 'lukewarm' and only fit to be spat out of the mouth of Christ. It is argued that this will be the state of the Church just prior to the Rapture.

They also take the view that the rapture of the Church will result in the turning of Israel to God en masse. Thus the role of Israel during the Millennium is to be the evangelists of the world. From this position, they argue that the events of Revelation exclusively relate to the nation of Israel. The gentile believers alluded to in Revelation (e.g. Revelation

6:9-11, Revelation 7:9-11 and Revelation 20:4) are those who are saved as a result of the activities of Israel during this period. The transition point is cited as being Revelation 4:1 where John hears a voice saying to him '"come up here and I will show you what must take place after these things."' In other words, John is seen here as being representative of the Church as he is called up into heaven.

For unbelievers left on earth, who observe the removal of the Church at the start of the Tribulation, this event will be seen as a mass and unexplained disappearance of people from the earth resulting in a generation of the 'left behind' some of whom will have been aware of the impending judgement and will, as a result, also turn to God. Scriptures such as Matthew 24:36-51 and Matthew 25:1-13 are used to support this view[10].

The merits and problems with the dispensational view are discussed in Chapter 3. Suffice to say for the moment that, whilst this view is attractive (and widely held amongst Evangelicals and Pentecostals) in that it gives the Church an 'escape clause', there are some serious issues with it both from a scriptural and from a logical viewpoint.

Will the Church be Triumphant at the Return of Christ?

If we take either the Post-millennial or A-Millennial view both of which minimise the Tribulation, the removal of the Church from the earth is seen as a gathering concurrent with the physical return of Christ to the earth. In other words, the rapture is an event during which the Church is caught up to meet Christ in the clouds (1 Thessalonians 4:16-17) on his return and it is during this event that the living and the dead are given their resurrection, incorruptible bodies (1 Corinthians 15:50-53). Also, it is at this time that the Church is transformed into a glorious bride and accompanies the groom on his descent to the earth.

Immediately before this event, particularly if we take the post-millennial view, the Church is seen as triumphant in the earth and, whilst it suffers through the period of Tribulation, is nevertheless seen as a 'bride made ready' (Revelation 19:7).

The degree to which this view is pursued vary; however, it is most fully

[10] *During the course of these studies the author read How Close Are We by Dave Hunt. His book presents a series of arguments in favour of a Pre-Tribulation Rapture. This view is propounded with the suggestion that anyone who does not accept it is mad, ignorant or stupid. To this end, I have dedicated Appendix 4 to a discussion of these arguments.*

developed in Restoration theology. Essentially, Restoration Theology[11] is based around the notion that God is restoring His Church to make it that which he had always intended it to be. In the latter days, just prior to the Second Coming of Christ, it will reach the place of maturity and will be a bride fit to meet the bridegroom. Each new movement since the days of the Reformation is identified as having restored some lost truth to the Church and, whilst each of these movements has resulted in a new denomination, which has not necessarily been helpful, the heritage of such restoration movements has been enjoyed by subsequent generations. Thus for example (and this list is not exhaustive):

- Lutherans restored Justification by Faith
- The Anabaptists restored believer's (or adult) baptism
- The Presbyterians restored plurality of leadership
- The Methodists restored the evangelistic thrust of the Church, taking the gospel onto the streets
- The Brethren restored the notion of the priesthood of all believers
- The Pentecostals restored the Baptism of the Spirit and the charismata
- The House Church Movement restored body ministry, cells and the present day reality of the Kingdom of God

This last element, an understanding of the Kingdom of God as a present reality rather than a future expectation (in contrast with this, Dispensational Theology puts the Kingdom of God off until the Millennium), is key to this theology. Thus, the time we are now in is the era in which the Kingdom of God will find its full expression in the world, culminating in the return of the King Himself to reign. Coupled with this is the notion that just prior to the return of Christ, the Church, having come through the process of restoration, and having spread throughout the whole earth, will exercise a governmental role in the earth on behalf of the king. Thus the Church is seen at the End Times as

[11] *Restoration theology was developed in the 1960's and 1970's and became the standard view-point of many charismatic fellowships and remains so to the present day. Essentially, it is post-millennial. Whilst it is not, to my knowledge, written down anywhere in any systematic form, it is often referred to by writers in the Charismatic churches. An example is in David Matthew's book Church Adrift where frequent reference is made to the end time church being 'resplendent in beauty, unity and maturity' (p.225)*

being Triumphant over the world, exercising a Godly influence over the human institutions and will be instrumental in ushering in a world-wide revival concluding with the Second Coming.

Scriptures used to enforce this view include Matthew 13:24-30, the Parable of the Wheat and the Tares, where we see the seeds sown by the enemy coming to fruition at the same time as the seeds sown by God. Hence, it is argued, the two Kingdoms will be at their strongest just before the End Times. Also, the Parable of the Mustard Seed (Matthew 13:31-35) which, from small beginnings, becomes a huge plant filling the whole earth and the Parable of the Yeast which works through the dough to transform it into bread are cited in support of this view.

Another scripture used is Daniel 3:44-45:

> *In the time of those kings, the God of heaven will set up a Kingdom that will never be destroyed, nor will it be left to another people. It will crush all those Kingdoms and bring them to an end, but it will itself endure forever. This is the meaning of the vision of the rock cut out of a mountain, but not by human hands - a rock that broke the iron, the bronze, the clay, the silver and the gold to pieces.*

From this passage it is argued that the Kingdom of God, the stone, will ultimately be triumphant in the earth over all earthly Kingdoms.

Restoration theology can be used to argue in favour of either a Post-Millennial or an A-Millennial position since, we could either say that we are in the Millennial reign of Christ now which will culminate in the Triumphant Church and the Return of Christ, or we could argue that there is no actual Millennial reign and that the return of Christ will simply be a time of transition from his spiritual to his physical reign on earth.

Are there any other options?

Clearly the Dispensational position is in direct conflict with the other position and all of them are based on scriptural inference rather than on direct and specific teaching on this subject. Either we see the End Time Church as triumphant or as lukewarm and apostate. However, Jesus himself was silent on both of these positions. He simply said in Luke 24:14:

And this gospel of the Kingdom will be preached in the whole world as a testimony to all nations, and then the end will come.

His emphasis is not on the Church being triumphant or apostate but simply on it continuing faithfully to preach the gospel until the work of preaching the gospel is finished (Revelation 10:7).

Summary

Following these diverse theological positions, we must conclude that either the church is absent during the Tribulation, leaving the work of spreading the gospel to Israel, or that it is present. The relative merits and demerits of these two views will be considered in the next chapter.

Chapter 3

The Millennium & the Rapture

Introduction

As with the view held on Israel, there has been much disagreement and controversy over the years concerning the occurrence of the Millennium and the rapture. In this chapter we will seek to discover the biblical position on these things, looking at some of the arguments for and against the various options and seeking to draw some conclusions as to the most tenable position.

The Millennium

Summary of the Millennium

The fundamental idea of the 'Millennium' is a period of history during which Christ reigns on earth, at the end of which will come the final judgement of Satan (following a short period in which he is released on the earth again) and the final judgement of the unbelievers who have died since the beginning of history.

Following this final judgement, the current heaven and earth will be discarded and a new heaven and a new earth created. The New

Jerusalem (all those Jews and Gentiles from the beginning of time who have put their faith in God) will descend from heaven and will be the dwelling place of God on the earth – this is symbolic and means that the only residents of the new earth will be believers of all ages who have entered into entire sanctification.

Problems with the Millennium

The following objections have been raised with respect to the occurrence of the Millennium

- It only appears in Revelation 20, which is a symbolic passage in a symbolic book and therefore, it is said, should not be taken literally.
- The Millennium infers a period on earth during which the perfect and the imperfect will live together. How can the perfect live in an imperfect world?
- The Millennium includes the celebration of the Feast of Booths (See Zechariah 14:9-21 which, whilst not mentioning 1000 years, speaks of the physical reign of God on the earth). Why should that particular feast continue?
- The Millennium infers the physical reign of Jesus from Jerusalem but, it is argued by A-Millennailists and Post-Millennialists, Jesus came to establish a spiritual kingdom, not a physical / temporal / political kingdom. They continue, God's purposes are with the Church, which has replaced physical Israel in the purposes of God and therefore there is not a need for Jesus to come and reign physically in Israel (see Chapter 1 above).

In response to these problems, 3 main schools of thought have emerged each of which we will consider throughout the remainder of this chapter.

A-Millennialism

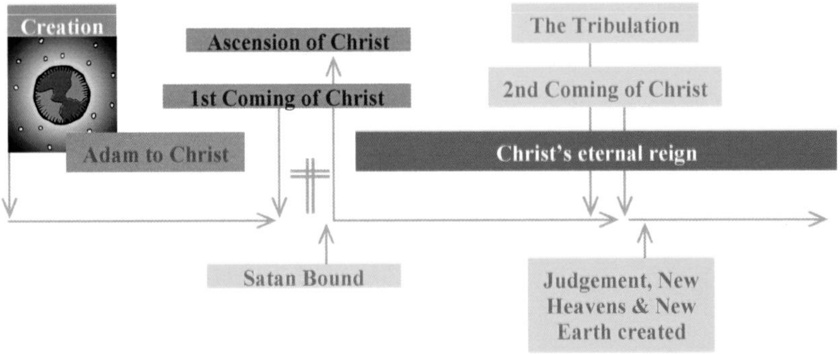

Summary of A-Millennialism

The a-millennial view is purely negative. It holds that there is no sufficient scriptural ground for the expectation of a Millennium and is firmly convinced that the Bible favours the idea that the present dispensation of the Kingdom of God will be followed immediately by the Kingdom of God in its consummate and eternal form. It is mindful of the fact that the Kingdom of Jesus Christ is represented as an eternal and not as a temporal Kingdom (Isaiah 9:7, Daniel 7:14, Luke 1:33, Heb 1:8, 12:28, 2 Peter 1:11, Rev 11:15), and to enter the Kingdom of the future is to enter upon one's eternal state (Matt 7:21-22); to enter life (Matt 18:8-9) and to be saved (Mark 10:25-26).

It interprets Revelation 20 symbolically, for example, the 'binding of Satan' happened as a result of Christ's redeeming work (Matthew 12:29) and, therefore, he is now limited in what he can do. The thousand-year reign is exercised not on earth but in heaven with Christ and refers to the gospel age between the two comings of Christ. Thus, the Millennium is not a literal period of history but a symbolic period during which Christ reigns through His church.

Objections to A-Millennialism

1. It ignores Revelation 20 or else rationalises it by assigning it to symbolism.
2. It ignores the Old Testament prophecies concerning a golden age for Israel (see below).
3. It ignores the literal covenants made with Abraham, Isaac, Jacob,

Moses & David by saying that they are only fulfilled spiritually in the Church (see Chapter 1 above).

4. It ignores the Messianic injunction that Jesus will reign on David's throne in that it teaches that the new heaven and the new earth will be created at the time of Christ's return. If this were to happen Jesus would never fulfil this Messianic prophecy.

Post-Millennialism

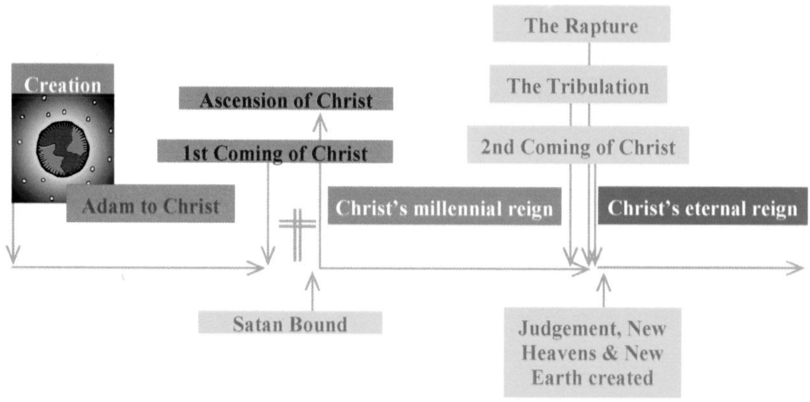

Summary of Post-Millennialism

The Post-millennial view is that Christ will return at the end of the Millennium, during which period the Church, and natural evolutionary development, will have ushered in a golden age. In other words the gospel, which will gradually spread through the whole world, will, in the end, become immeasurably more effective than it is at present, and will usher in a period of rich spiritual blessings for the Church of Jesus Christ, a golden age in which Jews will also share the blessings of the gospel in an unprecedented manner.

The 'golden age of the church' will be followed by a brief period of apostasy, a terrible conflict between the forces of good and evil, and by the simultaneous occurrence of the advent of Christ, the general resurrection and the final judgement.

It is post-millennialism which the Charismatic Movement has surreptitiously preached over the last 30 years whilst it has declared that the church will be triumphant in this age and will thus usher in the Kingdom in its full measure now.

Objections to Post Millennialism

1. The Church Triumphant in this age is not Scriptural.

The notion that

- the whole world will be won for Christ,
- that the life of all nations will be transformed by the gospel,
- that righteousness and peace will reign supreme prior to the return of Christ,
- that the blessings of the Spirit will be poured out in richer abundance than before so that the Church will experience a season of unexampled prosperity just before the coming of the Lord,
- all of this is not in harmony with the end of the ages as portrayed in scripture. Neither does it accord with the political development of the four empires, as will be seen in our studies in Daniel (see Chapter 5). In these studies it will become clear that the 'times of the gentiles', the period in which the political dominance of this world is in the hands of the gentile rulers whose mandate is to rule the whole World, will only come to an end at the Second Coming of Christ.

The Bible teaches that the gospel will spread throughout the whole world and will exercise a beneficent influence but does not lead us to expect the conversion of the whole world.

Matthew 24: 14 says, 'The gospel of the Kingdom shall be preached in the whole world as a testimony to all the nations, then the end will come'.

The Bible, in contrast to the Post-Millennial view, stresses the fact that the time just prior to the end will be a time of great apostasy (2 Thessalonians 2:3), of tribulation (Matthew 24:21) and persecution (Matthew 24:9), a time when the 'faith of many will grow cold' (Matthew 24:11) and when they who are loyal to

Christ will be subjected to bitter sufferings and will, in some cases, be martyred.

2. The Notion that the Cataclysmic Climax will not happen is not scriptural

The idea that the present age will not end in a great cataclysmic change but will pass almost imperceptibly into the coming age is equally unscriptural. The Bible teaches us explicitly that a catastrophe, a special intervention of God, involving his judgement being poured out upon the earth, will bring the rule of Satan on earth to an end, and will usher in the Kingdom that cannot be shaken (Matt 24:29-31, 35-44, Heb 12:26-27, 2 Peter 3:10-13).

Pre-Millennialism

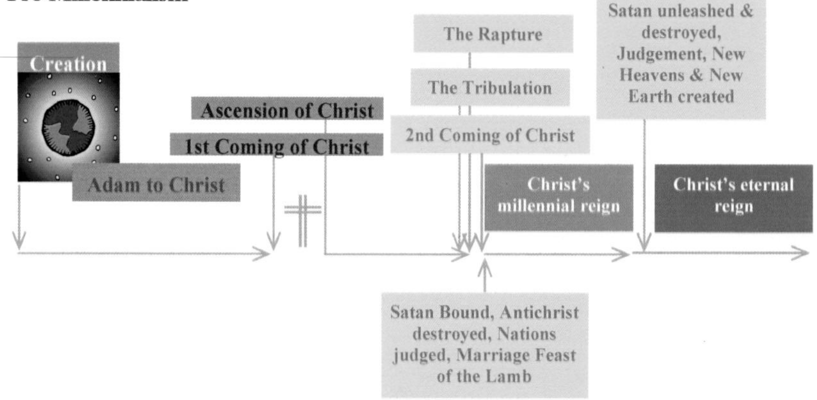

Pre-millennialism infers the return of Christ prior to his millennial reign on earth. Historically, it has been closely associated with Dispensationalism, although the two are not mutually dependent.

In summary, it argues that the current age will continue until, in the last days prior to the return of Christ, the Antichrist will arise and the Jews and believers who are on the earth at that time will be persecuted and martyred. Finally, Christ will return, defeat Satan and place him in 'the abyss' (Revelation 20:1). He will have the Antichrist and the false prophet thrown into the lake of fire, judge the nations, and set up his 1000-year reign on the earth.

Most Pre-Millennialists would agree with this summary. The problems arise over the timing of the rapture.

Objections to Pre-Millennialism

1. The only clear passage spelling out a thousand year reign is in Revelation 20. If this whole passage is taken literally then the only people involved in the Millennial Reign are beheaded martyrs, unless they are seen as representative of all the saints (Revelation 20:4-5).
2. Events seen in Revelation 20 as happening on either side of the Millennium, such as the Judgement of Unbelievers, are in other passages seen as happening concurrently (Daniel 12:2, Matthew 13:37-42, 47-50, 24:29-31, 25:31-46, Acts 24:15, Revelation 20:11-15).

We either have to assume that the one thousand years after Christ returns is symbolic of his post-return reign, or else we have to try and find work-arounds for the above problems.

Let us now consider the three positions which Pre-Millennialists take regarding the timing of the rapture.

The Rapture

Pre-Tribulation Rapture

Those who advocate a pre-Tribulation rapture (i.e. the removal of the Church just prior to the last 7 years of human history) declare that the Church will be removed from the earth before the Antichrist arises (both the film 'Thief in the Night' and the 'Left Behind' series are based on this theological position). The result will be that amongst those left behind, there will be a turning to Christ, including the whole nation of Israel, who will become the evangelists of the world, bringing salvation to 'the multitude' of Revelation 7:9-17 during the Tribulation. Thus, they will be the focus of the persecution of the Antichrist.

After a period of 7 years, Christ will return (as above) and set up His

Millennial Kingdom. The Millennial Kingdom will exclusively involve Israel – during the Tribulation, the Church will be away enjoying the Marriage Supper of the Lamb and will not be involved at all. It is not clear what the Church will be doing during the Millennium except 'reigning with Christ' in some way.

Problems with Pre-Tribulation rapture:

1. It is not stated explicitly in scripture anywhere. Rather it is an inference that has been drawn based on the doctrinal pre-disposition that the Tribulation and the Millennial Kingdom exclusively involve Israel and, therefore, it has been constructed as a device to remove the Church from the picture so that this can happen.
2. It infers two comings of Jesus: one for the Church and one for the Kingdom. However, all scriptures that talk about the coming of the Lord do so in the singular form – there is no mention of two Second Comings.
3. In Matthew 24:31, Jesus explicitly positions the gathering of the 'elect' as occurring at his coming – a coming that 'all the tribes of the earth' will see. The only way around this is to make the assumption that the gathering of 'the elect' here means the gathering of Israel, however, this is contrary to Paul's use of the word 'elect' in Romans 8:33. Also compare 2 Thessalonians 2:1-3 where 'our gathering together to Him' is positioned very specifically after the revealing of the 'man of lawlessness'.
4. Revelation 5:9-10, speaking of the Church, clearly states that the Church will reign upon earth. If the Church is not involved in the Millennial Kingdom, this can only happen in the new heaven and the new earth, however, this does not fit in with the flow of the rest of Revelation.
5. It is argued by Pre-Tribulation exponents that Old Testament passages concerning the Millennial Kingdom are seen as exclusive to Israel (Micah 4-5, Obadiah v.15-21, Amos 9:11-15, Joel 3:18-21, Hosea 2:14-23, Zephaniah 3:12-20, Zechariah 8, 10, 14:9-21, Isaiah 60-66, Jeremiah 31, 33, Ezekiel 37:24-28. 39:25-29 and numerous other passages). Whilst there is no doubt that these passages refer primarily to Israel, they are not exclusive. If we follow the same argument, we would have to say that from

the Old Testament passages alone, the salvation made available under the New Covenant is only for Israel since only Israel are explicitly mentioned regarding the salvation of God in these passages (for example, Jeremiah 33:31-34[12]). Thus, following the same logic, we would exclude all Gentiles (including ourselves) from any of the blessings associated with the cross. However, the whole thrust of Paul's argument in Ephesians 2 and 3 is that God's purpose is not ultimately to have two sets of people through whom he is working out His purposes, but one. The Second Coming will be the time when that unification takes place, when Israel will look upon him 'whom they have pierced' (Zechariah 12:10), and turn en masse back to God, and Christ will bring back with him the resurrected and raptured, glorified saints (1 Thessalonians 3:13). Israel will not come to God through a further covenant but through the covenant already inaugurated in Jesus. In contrast with dispensational views, there is no further covenant to come. He (Jesus) is God's last word for salvation! (See Hebrews 10:1-18).

Mid-Tribulation Rapture

Some advocate that the rapture happens halfway through the Tribulation. Passages used to infer this are 2 Thessalonians 2:7, Daniel 7:25. In other words, they argue that the rapture of the Church occurs when the Holy Spirit is removed from the world, which occurs just prior to the Antichrist coming to the height of his power, which occurs 3 ½ years into the Tribulation.

The argument against a mid-Tribulation rapture revolves around who or what is 'the restraining influence' in 2 Thessalonians 2:7. There are actually three options here:

1. The restrainer is the Holy Spirit whose activities counteract evil influences.
2. The restraining influence is the preaching of the gospel (although the context gives no indication of this).
3. The restraining influence is political government. Paul had in mind the restraining influence of the Roman Empire on warring factions, summed up in the person of the emperor. In our studies

[12] *Commenting on this in Hebrews 8:7-13, the writer to the Hebrews states clearly that this New Covenant has been inaugurated through the death and resurrection of Jesus and therefore there cannot be a better covenant still to come.*

> in Daniel (Chapter 6) it will be shown that the Antichrist will sweep aside all other power and take over the running of the world directly. Thus, the restraining influence of government, democracy etc. will be swept aside in order for the Antichrist to arise.

Pre-Tribulation and Mid-Tribulation Pre-Millennialists try to differentiate the 'coming of the Lord' from 'the day of the Lord' (1 Thessalonians 4:15, 5:1). Thus, the Coming of the Lord is associated with the rapture and the Day of the Lord with his judgement. Clearly, within all passages concerning the Second Coming these terms are used interchangeably and any attempt to suggest that the two are separate is to make mincemeat of the text.

The most likely interpretation concerning the identification of the 'restraining influence' is the third of the above. Whichever of these options we choose, however, this passage cannot be used to support a pre-Tribulation rapture since it is clear from it and from our studies in Daniel (see chapters 5-7), that the Antichrist will not come into his full power until half way through the Tribulation and will rule for 3 ½ years. Thus, if we say that the removal of the Holy Spirit from the world has to happen in order for the Antichrist to be revealed, this event can only happen half way through the Tribulation and therefore, at best, the rapture can only happen half way through the Tribulation and not before.

It is tenuous, to say the least, to use this verse as a sole justification for a mid-Tribulation rapture and therefore we will lay it aside taking instead what Scripture says clearly about the rapture.

Post-Tribulation Rapture

If we dismiss the notion of a pre or mid-Tribulation rapture, we are left with a post-Tribulation rapture. In other words, the Church as well as Israel will go through the Tribulation, at the end of which Christ will return. At this point, 'the dead in Christ will rise first and be caught up with Him in the clouds'. Those believers who are left alive at His coming will then also be caught up with Him and will at that moment be transformed and given their resurrection bodies (1 Corinthians 15:52). They will then descend with him to the earth and reign with him in his Millennial Kingdom (Daniel 7:27, Revelation 5:9-10, Matthew 25:14-30).

The following passages, when read in their most literal form support this view: Matthew 24, Luke 24, 1 Corinthians 15:12-28, 50-57, 1 Thessalonians 4:13-18, 5:1-11, 2 Thessalonians 2:1-3.

A problem with this view is that if the saints alive on earth at the coming of the Lord are raptured and that on Jesus' arrival on earth, Israel are saved en masse, are Israel glorified along with the rest of the saints or do they remain in their mortal bodies until they die? If, as has been argued, God's purpose is to make the two (Jew & Gentile believers) one at that point in time, how can they be one if some are glorified and some are not? This is problematic and there is no clear answer to this problem.

Conclusion

Given the above arguments, the position taken by the author concerning the Millennium and the rapture is Post-Tribulation Pre-Millennial. From the information given above and from further study, the reader is welcome to make up their own mind, however, much of the material considered below from the apocalyptic and prophetic scriptures will be analysed from this viewpoint.

Chapter 4

The Second Coming

Introduction

Once more, there has been much disagreement and controversy over the years concerning the events surrounding the Second Coming of Christ. On one side we have the Jehovah's Witnesses saying that the Second Coming has already happened but could only be seen with the eye of faith. On the other hand we have those who work with charts and plans trying to decide exactly when and how it will occur.

In this chapter we will seek to discover the biblical position on the Second Coming of Christ and the events surrounding it.

The Second Coming & the Rapture

There are a number of different words used in the various passages which describe the Second Coming, each of which brings its own nuance to the events of that time:

- the Harpazo (literally, 'Snatching up' or 'seizing with force' – 1 Thessalonians 4:17);
- the Episunagoge (literally, 'gathering' – Matthew 24:31,

2 Thessalonians 2:1);
- the Parousia ('coming' or literally 'presence' – 1 Corinthians 15:23, 1 Thessalonians 2:19, 3:13,4:15, 5:23, 2 Thessalonians 2:1&8);
- Apokalypsis (literally, 'revelation' – 2 Thessalonians 1:7, 1 Corinthians 1:7, 3:13);
- the epiphaneia (literally, 'appearing' or 'manifestation' – 2 Thessalonians 2:8, Titus 2:13 – this also carries with it the notion of drawing back a veil so that what is already there may be truly seen for what it is).

Essentially, these words taken together betray two elements: firstly, a snatching up and gathering together of the saints, and secondly, the sudden appearing or revelation of Christ. In these passages, there is no gap between these events: they occur together.

This is made particularly clear in Matthew 24:29-31, Mark 13:24-17: 'Immediately after the Tribulation of those days….they will see the SON OF MAN COMING ON THE CLOUDS OF THE SKY…and he will send forth His angels with a GREAT TRUMPET and THEY WILL GATHER TOGETHER His elect from the four winds, from one end of the sky to the other.' Jesus is seen at the time when he gathers his elect together. Pre-Millennialists would argue that the 'elect here' means Israel, however, this would suggest a supernatural re-gathering of Israel when Jesus returns which is not supported elsewhere in scripture.

In the same passage as the coming of Jesus is portrayed (Matthew 24:40-41), we see the rapture occurring. The context of the rapture is thus 'the coming of the Son of Man' (v.39 cf. v.30). This is confirmed again in 1 Corinthians 15:21-28: '…those who are Christ's at his coming, then comes the end…' (Cf. Philippians 3:20-21) and in 1 Corinthians 15:51-53: 'The Last Trumpet will sound…' (Compare Revelation 11:15ff).

1 Thessalonians 4:13-18 says, 'God will bring with Him those who have fallen asleep in Jesus….For the Lord will descend from heaven with a shout, with the voice of the archangel and with the trumpet of God and the dead in Christ will rise first. Then we who are alive and remain will be caught up together with them in the clouds to meet the Lord in the air…', and will descend to earth with him '…at the coming of the Lord Jesus with all His saints' (1 Thessalonians 3:13).

The whole thrust of these passages is that at Jesus' coming the church will be caught up to be with him and will be transformed and given immortal bodies. She will meet Him in the clouds and return to earth with him in a transformed state and thus will 'always be with him' and will reign with him.

The Coming of Christ

The following statements concerning the Parousia can be made categorically, without dispute on the basis of scripture.

1. It will be a personal Coming
In Acts 1:11, the angels who appeared to the disciples at the occasion of Christ's ascension stated, 'This Jesus, who has been taken up from you into heaven will come in just the same way as you have watched Him go into heaven'. In other words, Jesus will come again in person, in His glorified state.

2. It will be a physical coming
Jesus will return to earth in body, (Acts 1:11, 3:20-21, Hebrews 9:28, Revelation 1:7). It will not be a coming for those who see him with the eye of faith. He will come to the earth in a physical body and will reign physically on the earth.

3. It will be a visible coming
His appearance will not be just for those with the eye of faith: 'Every eye will see Him' (Matthew 24:30, 26:64, Mark 13:26, Luke 21:27, Acts 1:11, Colossians 3:4, Titus 2:13, Hebrews 9:28, Revelation 1:7).

4. It will be a sudden coming
The Bible teaches that the Second Coming will be preceded by certain signs but it also teaches that, for those who don't know Him, it will be unexpected and sudden (Matthew 24:37-44, 25:1-12, Mark 13:33-37, 1 Thessalonians 5:2-3, Revelation 3:3, 16:15). This is considered in more detail in chapter 13 & 14 which consider the teaching of the End Times in the New Testament.

5. It will be a glorious and triumphant coming

He will not come as a babe, as in his first advent but as a conquering king. Thus it will be very different from His first coming:

- He will come in a glorified body (Hebrews 9:28)
- The clouds of heaven will be His chariot (Matthew 24:30)
- The angels will be His bodyguards (2 Thessalonians 1:7)
- The archangels will be His heralds (1 Thessalonians 4:16)
- The saints of God will be His glorious retinue (1 Thessalonians 3:13, 2 Thessalonians 1:10)
- He will come as King of Kings and Lord of Lords, triumphant over all the forces of evil, having put all His enemies under His feet (1 Corinthians 15:25, Revelation 19:11-16).

Section 2

The Prophetic/Apocalyptic Scriptures

Chapter 5

Studies in Daniel: The Rise of Empires I

Introduction

In the book of Daniel, a number of visions occur, revealed either directly to Daniel or to those he was serving at the time. These visions give us a picture of the future from Daniel's perspective and map out some of the critical events of world history, right through to the return of Christ, as we shall see. As we examine the visions individually and collectively, this view of the future will emerge and will form the framework for our study of the apocalyptic and prophetic scriptures as they relate to the End Times. However, before we study the visions, let us first try and discover who Daniel was.

From the evidence contained within the book of Daniel itself, he was a member of the Jewish nobility (Daniel 1:3) taken captive during the first Babylonian conquest of Jerusalem in 605 BC (Daniel 1:1).

This first captivity occurred when Nebuchadnezzar, king of Babylon, came up against Jerusalem and conquered it on his way back from defeating the Egyptians (during which campaign, Nebuchadnezzar's father, Nabopolassar, founder of the Chaldean Empire, had died). Jehoiakim was King of Judah at the time and remained so for a further 8 years until, foolishly, he rebelled against Nebuchadnezzar and so the Babylonian king sent a task force to kill him, which they successfully did in 597 BC (2 Kings 24:1-6). It was at this time that some of the other members of the nobility were taken to Babylon (see Daniel 1:1-3).

Jehoikim's son, Jehoiachin, became the King of Judah, for a further 3 months, during which time Jerusalem was under siege. The siege was ended when Jehoiachin gave himself up and was taken captive by Nebuchadnezzar, along with the royal family and most of the remaining nobles. These were all deported to Babylon, along with the treasures of the Temple, the craftsmen and the fighting men (see 2 Kings 24:10-16), and Jehoiachin's uncle, Zedekiah was put on the throne of Judah as a puppet king. This happened around the year 597 BC. Zedekiah remained on the throne for a further eleven years until he too rebelled. At that time, Nebuchadnezzar came against Jerusalem and flattened it completely, destroying the Temple and the city walls. Thus it remained until the restoration, the rebuilding of the temple finally being completed around 516 BC.

As a result of the above events, Daniel and his compatriots (Hananiah, Mishael, and Azariah), all of noble birth, found themselves in the Babylonian King's service. They were probably aged between 16 and 20 when they arrived in Babylon and were educated in the Babylonian universities so that they might serve the king as civil servants or in some other capacity. It is also likely that they would have been made eunuchs to fulfil this role.

Daniel, himself, was a man of integrity and of unswerving commitment to His God, despite the seductions of the Babylonian religions which surrounded him every day. This is made clear in Daniel 1:8-17, where Daniel and his friends insist on maintaining a simple lifestyle and diet in order that they would 'not defile' themselves, despite the fact that this course of action could have resulted in them being dismissed from the king's service or even killed.

We also know that they successfully passed through their training period and entered the king's service (Daniel 1:18-21) and that Daniel continued in some function throughout the era of the Babylonian empire, through to the reign of Cyrus, the first Medo-Persian king (known in antiquity as Cyrus the Great). For a list of the various Babylonian kings, through to the overthrow of the dynasty by Cyrus see Appendix 1.

For external verification of the life of Daniel, we can refer to the book of Jeremiah where independent reference is given of him. Also, the writings of Josephus give brief details of his life. Finally, we have the existence of the shrine of Daniel in Susa (southern Iran), which is widely venerated by the Arabs of the Iranian Khuzestan, by the Iranian Muslims, by Jews and by Christians.

The Visions of the book of Daniel

The book of Daniel contains a number of visions, which define in significant detail the events which would occur, both in the immediate years following these visions, and in the subsequent period leading up to the coming in power of 'the Son of Man' (Daniel 7:13-14).

Within this study, we will consider the following visions:

1. The Vision of Nebuchadnezzar (Daniel 2:31-43) which occurred between 605 and 598 BC when Daniel was between 15 and 22 years old.
2. The Vision of the Four Beasts (Daniel 7:1-8) which occurred in 553 BC when Daniel was 67 years old.
3. The Vision of the Ram and the Goat (Daniel 8: 1-8) which occurred in 551 BC when Daniel was 69 years old.
4. The Angelic Visitation - the 70 weeks (Daniel 9: 24-27) which occurred in 539 BC when Daniel was 81 years old.

In addition, when we come to consider the person of the Antichrist and the final years in subsequent chapters, we will also consider parts of Daniel chapters 11 and 12.

Summary of the Visions

Whilst the visions given are all unique and are received at various times during Daniel's life, there is a tremendous correlation and harmony between them, and together they build a composite picture of the future. This will be demonstrated as we consider these visions in detail below.

The First Vision

The first vision appears in Daniel chapter 2 and is given by God to Nebuchadnezzar. Daniel 2:28-29 tells us that whilst the king is considering the future of his Kingdom, God reveals to him what will take place both concerning his Kingdom and in the future.

In the vision, Nebuchadnezzar sees a statue with a head of gold, chest and arms of silver, belly and thighs of bronze and legs of iron and feet of iron and clay. Daniel interprets the various parts of the statue as representing four successive Kingdoms which were to arise in the earth. The culmination of the vision is the establishment of a final Kingdom by 'the God of Heaven' (v.44) which would shatter all of the previous Kingdoms and would 'endure forever'.

This first vision gives us a summary of The Times of the Gentiles[13] (see Luke 21:24) which takes us through to the end of time, when God's Kingdom will come physically and politically (as opposed to its current spiritual manifestation) with the return of Christ to establish a time/ space governmental Kingdom on earth.

This vision was revealed to Nebuchadnezzar and is therefore human history from man's perspective.

The Second Vision

The second vision is contained in Daniel chapter 7. Essentially, Daniel sees four great beasts coming out of the 'great sea' (Mediterranean). The first is like a lion with 'the wings of an eagle'; the second is like a lop-sided bear; the third is like a leopard with four wings on its back and four heads; the fourth is indescribable except that it is extremely terrifying and has ten horns and large iron teeth.

The second vision, in giving us a description of each of the four Kingdoms, reveals the essential nature of those Kingdoms - something of their character. If we have any doubt about what these four beasts represent, the angelic interpretation, given in verses 15-27 of chapter 7 tells us clearly that the four beasts represent four Kingdoms (v.17 & 23). It is safe to assume that these four Kingdoms correlate with the four Kingdoms of the first vision since, in that vision, only four are perceived

---

[13] *The Times of the Gentiles is defined as a period in history during which various kings and world leaders are given the authority to rule over the whole earth. This period began with Nebuchadnezzar and will end with the return of Christ.*

as arising before the coming of the Kingdom of God. In the same way, the interpretation of this vision concludes with God reigning in sovereign power (v.27) following the rise of four Kingdoms.

In that the Beasts come up out of the sea, this is symbolic of the gentile nations (cf. Is 17:12-13, Matt 13:47-60, Rev 13:1, 17:1&15) and tells us that these Kingdoms are gentile Kingdoms. The winds of heaven indicate God's sovereign purpose being worked out in the earth - the empires arise out of God's sovereign plan.

This vision is received by Daniel but interpreted by an angel and is therefore God's perspective on human history. There are actually four visions in this passage (v.2-6, v.7-8, v.912 and v.13-14) and each follows on directly from the previous one.

The Third Vision

In the third vision (Daniel 8:1-27), Daniel sees a confrontation between a lopsided ram and a goat with a 'conspicuous horn between his eyes', where the goat overwhelms the ram completely.

The third vision gives us some specific details of the confrontation between the second and third of these Kingdoms. We do not have to go far to find the interpretation of this vision since it is contained within the chapter itself. What is made clear is that the ram represents the Medo-Persian empire (v.20), and the goat represents 'the Kingdom of Greece' (v.21).

The First Angelic Visitation

In Daniel chapter 9, Daniel is praying specifically concerning the restoration of his people to the land of Israel, having observed from the book of Jeremiah that the restoration would come 70 years after the exile (Jeremiah 19:10). In response to his prayer, an angel comes to Daniel and gives him specific information concerning a period of history covered by seventy weeks (or seventy weeks of years to be specific), which would include the coming of the Messiah (Daniel 8:25). We will return to this visitation in chapter 7.

The Second Angelic Visitation

Chapters 10 to 12 of the book of Daniel contain details of the final angelic visitation received by Daniel. Much of the information imparted to him during this time relates to the conflicts during the inter-testamental years. However, the latter part of chapter 11 and chapter 12 of Daniel deal specifically with the End Times. Again, we will return to these passages in Chapter 7.

The Kingdoms Considered

Drawing upon the first three visions outlined above, we will now consider the Kingdoms which, according to the revelation received, would arise in the earth.

1. Babylon

From the first vision, revealed in Daniel 2:36-38, clearly the first Kingdom is Babylon ('You O king ….are the head of gold' v.37). It is also made clear in this vision that it was given to Babylon to rule over the whole earth: 'wherever the sons of men dwell or the beasts of the field, or the birds of the sky, He has given them into your hand and has caused you to rule over them all'. We know from history that Nebuchadnezzar did not exercise this right. In fact of all the empires described in these passages, his was the smallest. However, the suggestion is that he could have gone further had he so chosen (cf. Jeremiah 27:5-7).

Also from this vision, we have the suggestion that there is something superior about the Babylonian Kingdom compared to the others. In the vision, the value of the metals decreases the further down the statue we go. Babylon is represented by the most precious of the metals of the time, gold - a regal material associated with kingship throughout the ages.

This could be interpreted in various ways; however the suggestion is (as will be developed below) that this represents the highest form of government from a certain perspective. Absolute monarchy existed in the Babylonian society - the king was the law. Whilst we, with our western mindset might consider this the lowest form of government, associated with despots throughout the ages, God's perspective is different from ours, since absolute monarchy is the closest form of government to his own. God is an absolute ruler: his word is law. However, his rulership is typified by grace, mercy and love. He is a benign dictator, but a dictator nonetheless. We do not have the option to stand against his rule, and ultimately, all rebellion will be judged and judged severely.

Whilst accepting fully that Nebuchadnezzar was a fallen man who clearly became proud and arrogant in his rule (Daniel 3&4), the form of government he exercised was similar to that exercised by God himself. For those who served him well, he reserved 'gifts and a reward and great honour'(1:6); for those who did not serve him well or upset him, the punishment was that he would tear them 'limb from limb' and make their house a 'rubbish heap' (1:5, 3:29).

Nebuchadnezzar built the regal splendour of Babylon including the Hanging Gardens which became one of the ancient Wonders of the World. We are not exactly sure what the hanging gardens were since knowledge of them has only come down to us through later descriptions[14]. The suggestion is that Nebuchadnezzar had a wife who was from the southerly mountainous regions of the country. Thus, to make her feel more at home, he had a 'mountain' built in the city. This mountain was watered by mechanical irrigation devices and was populated with exotic plants.

We will never know for sure, but what is clear from writers such as Herodatus is that the splendour and wealth of Babylon was great indeed.

We also know that Nebuchadnezzar was ruthless. If this is not clear from the description of him in Daniel, an example from history is his treatment of some of his army officers who rebelled against him in 595 BC. He put down their rebellion fiercely and had many of his army officers executed.

In the second vision, recorded in Daniel 7:4, Babylon is described as being like a lion (king of beasts), with eagle's wings (king of birds). The winged lion was the symbol of Babylon and can still be seen on the reconstructions of the Ishtar Gate. This imagery is used elsewhere in scripture concerning Babylon: Lion – Jeremiah 50:17 & 44; Eagle – Jeremiah 49:17-22, Ezekiel 17:3.

In the vision, the lion loses its wings, and begins to walk upright, and to talk and reason like a man. The wings speak of speedy travel in order to conquer. In keeping with this vision, after establishing his Kingdom, Nebuchadnezzar ceased from further conquest, settled

[14] *See Appendix 5.*

back in regal pleasure, and developed Babylon into a place of learning. At this point the Babylonians began to pursue and build a higher more humane society.

2. Medo-Persian Empire

The first vision (Daniel 2:39) passes over the Medo-Persian empire very speedily with the remark 'after you there will arise another Kingdom inferior to you'. More detail is given concerning this empire in the second and third visions.

In summary, the Medo-Persian Empire took over the Babylonian Empire in 539BC, the same night as the events related in Daniel 5, where extended New Year revelries ended in disaster for the acting king Belshazzar[15].

Cyrus, the Medo-Persian king, defeated Babylon and appointed Darius (Gobryas) as prince of the Babylonian province, whom Daniel was appointed to serve. It was Darius who put Daniel in the Lion's den at the age of 85 in Daniel chapter 6.

Returning to the vision, we see that the chest and arms of the statue, which represent the Medo-Persian Empire, were of silver. This indicates that, although the Persian Emperor was very powerful, the emperor was not an absolute ruler. He was subject to 'The Law of the Medes and Persians', (see Daniel 6:15 and also Xerxes in the book of Esther who cannot revoke a previous law but allows Mordecai to write a law to countermand it (Esther 8:8)). This was an oligarchy.

We also see in Daniel 2:39 that the same domain was given to the Medo-Persian Empire as had been given to Babylon, namely, to rule 'over all the earth'. The Medo-Persian Empire did extend in all directions beyond the Babylonian empire and included the lands to the east of Babylon. Essentially, it covered the modern day regions of Iran, Iraq, Syria, Turkey (south of the Hellespont), Jordan, Israel, and also exacted hegemony over the neighbouring states such as Egypt.

In Daniel 7:5, this empire is depicted as being like a bear, 'raised up on one side'. It is unbalanced or lopsided in that although the Medes were longer established as a people, they had formed an alliance with the Persians to help defeat the Assyrians in 612 BC, after being

[15] *See Appendix 5.*

defeated by the Persians. The three ribs in the bear's mouth represent the three Kingdoms which had been defeated to establish the Medo-Persian Empire, namely, Babylonia, Lydia and Egypt. Later, further conquests were made including the brief occupation of Greece following the famous battle with the Greeks at Thermopylae, under Xerxes (Esther's husband).

A bear defeats its enemies by sheer force. In the same way, the Medo-Persians defeated their enemies by amassing huge armies by which they overcame through sheer weight of numbers (between ½ million and 2 ½ million depending whose accounts you choose to believe).

In the third vision (Daniel 8:3-4, 20) the Medo-Persian Empire is described as a Ram, which was the zodiacal symbol for Persia (Aries). Also, the ram's horn was worn on the head of a Persian king when going into battle. The horns of the ram in the vision are odd like the arms of the bear confirming the lopsided nature of the balance of power between the Medes and the Persians.

The ram butted its way north, south and west (these relate to the three ribs of the previous vision). No one could stand against it (8:4). The Medo-Persians did suffer some defeats against the Greeks, first at the Battle of Marathon under Darius the Great, and second at the battle of Salamis under Xerxes (they were withheld for several days at the battle of Thermopylae until the Greeks were betrayed by one of their own), however, they did occupy Greece for a time until they became tired of fighting and went home.

We are also told in the vision (v.4) that this empire became proud of itself. At the Battle of Thermopylae, Xerxes just expected the Greeks to surrender to him. Instead, 300 Spartans and some soldiers from other Greek city states withheld him and his army to the death and killed thousands of Persians in so doing.

Ultimately this empire was succeeded by the third empire.

3. The Greek Empire

Similar to the reference to the Medo-Persian empire, the third empire is passed over swiftly in the first vision with the words, 'then a third Kingdom of bronze which will rule over all the earth' (Daniel 2: 39). Again, we will add in more details concerning this empire when we consider the other visions. Suffice to say that this vision refers to the Hellenistic Empire of Greece and Macedonia established under Alexander the Great.

In the vision, the belly and thighs of the statue are made of bronze. In the Greek form of monarchy there was no dynasty as such – the one who conquered ruled. Alexander received the Kingdom from his father Philip of Macedon, who had conquered and united the city states of Greece and Macedonia. On his, death, Alexander assumed the throne and disposed of any would be contenders. Following Alexander's death, the empire was divided up amongst his four generals (see below). Headship in this empire was by rule of conquest.

In the vision, the same mandate of 'dominion' was given to the Greek empire as was given to Babylon (Daniel 7:6), to rule over the whole earth. In other words, the Greeks could have gone further but didn't[16]. Alexander wanted to push on over the Indus River and conquer the southern plains of India but his army refused to go with him. It was soon after this that he returned to Babylon and drank himself into an early grave.

In the second vision (Daniel 7:6), the Greek Empire is depicted as a leopard with four wings. This symbolises swiftness of attack – the Greek empire was built in 10 years during which time Alexander conquered Eastern Europe, Asia, North Africa and Northern India, all the way to the Indus River. Also, during this time, he utterly destroyed the power of the Persian Empire which, up until this point, had been the world superpower.

The four heads in this vision symbolise the 4 Greek generals who supported Alexander and took over the Empire after he died, namely, Lysimachus, Cassander, Ptolemy, and Seleucus.

[16] *'There were plans, it was rumoured. There was, for example, an astonishing document, which came into the hands of Diodorus Siculus, listing them. This document probably owed its origin to the secretary Eumenes (Perhaps it was noted down during the king's last moments of lucidity that sweltering June in Babylon, in the times the fever abated?) These were Alexander's plans:*
'First military: the conquest of Arabia; the building of 1000 extra large warships for a campaign to take Carthage and the western Mediterranean; the building of a military road all the way across North Africa from Alexandria to Gibraltar with harbours, bases, and arsenals. None of this is implausible, much of it widely attested in the tradition. Alexander certainly planned to conquer the West, perhaps 'even as far as the Britannic Isles', as Arrian said....'

Quoted from 'In the Footsteps of Alexander The Great', p.234 by Michael Wood

In the third vision, related in Daniel 8:5-8, Greece is symbolised by a goat. This was the Zodiacal sign for Greece (Capricorn) and would have been a familiar image to the audience of the book of Daniel. In addition, Alexander wore the horns of a goat on his head and even today in places such as Iraq, he is known as 'the two horned one'.

In the vision, the goat charges to attack. This gives indication of speed once again. The 'conspicuous horn' between its eyes is Alexander the Great (see v.21). He was born in 356 BC. His father was Philip of Macedon, who united the tribes of Greece and Macedonia in order to fight the Persians, but was murdered (Alexander's mother and possibly Alexander himself were implicated in Philip's assassination). Alexander was educated by Aristotle and took over from his father in 336 BC aged 20. Two years later he went against the Persians who were much stronger than the Greek army (Alexander set out from Macedonia with only 35,000 troops). The Greeks had never forgiven the Persians for invading Greece in 480BC under Xerxes and wanted revenge for Thermopylae. Because of this desire for vengeance they were 'enraged' (v.7).

In Daniel 8:7, the goat strikes the ram, shatters his horns and hurls him to the ground. This relates to the three significant battles between the Greeks and the Persians:

a. The Persians were 'struck' at the Battle of Granicus River in May 334, which resulted in the liberation of the Greek cities of Asia Minor from Persian control.
b. The Greeks 'shattered the horns' of the Persians at the Battle of Issus in November 333 BC, dividing its power base from the Mediterranean (Phoenician) and Egyptian parts of its empire, before heading south thereby breaking the horns in a crushing defeat, taking away the empire status of the Persians.
c. The Persians were 'hurled to the ground and trampled...' at the Battle of Guagamela in October 331 BC where the Greeks defeated the Kingdom altogether, sacking its cities (including the complete destruction of the winter Capital, Susa) and taking over its territories.

Daniel 8:8 finishes with the words 'then the male goat magnified himself exceedingly. But as soon as he was mighty, the large horn was broken; and in its place there came up four conspicuous horns toward the four winds of heaven.'

In pride, (he had written to Athens to request that he be proclaimed a god), at the height of his power, aged 32, Alexander died of drunkenness (or possibly he was poisoned) in June 323 BC. The empire was then divided amongst his four generals:

a. Lysimachus took Thrace and Bithynia (North)
b. Cassander took Macedonia and Greece (West)
c. Ptolemy took Egypt, Palestine and Edom (South - it was from Ptolemy that Cleopatra was descended).
d. Seleucus took Syria, Babylonia and the East to the Indus River.

Verses 9 to 14 and 23 to 26 of Daniel 8 refer to a descendent of one of Alexander's generals, known as Antiochus Epiphanes, who is a type of the Antichrist. We will consider these passages in some detail in chapter 7.

This dividing of Alexander's empire is confirmed a further time in Daniel 11:3-4. Of those directly related to Alexander who might have assumed the throne, his mistress, Barsine and her son Heracles were killed; Roxanne, his eastern wife, and her son survived until 313 BC when they were murdered; Alexander's second wife, Stateira, the daughter of Darius, was killed by Roxanne. Even Alexander's mother, Olympias, was killed in a civil war in Macedonia.

Thus the visions of Daniel were literally fulfilled in the first three great empires of The Times of the Gentiles. We will consider the fourth empire in the next chapter.

Summary

In this chapter we have identified the first three empires which were to arise in the earth during the period known as 'the times of the gentiles', and as detailed in the book of Daniel. These empires are: Babylon, Medo-Persia and Greece. In the following chapter, we will consider the fourth of these empires.

Chapter 6

Studies in Daniel: The Rise of Empires II

Summary of the visions of Daniel

In the previous chapter, we considered the visions of Daniel contained in chapters 2, 7 and 8 of the book of Daniel. The following summarises our learning from this study:

- In Daniel 2 we considered the statue of Gold, Silver, Bronze, Iron / Iron-clay which was said to represent four empires in terms of their value and governmental style.
- In Daniel 7 we considered the four creatures which were said to represent four empires in terms of their nature, being the empires of Babylonia, Medo-Persia, Greece and a fourth empire, as yet undisclosed.
- In Daniel 8, we considered the conflict between the Ram and the Goat and saw how this matched how the Greek Empire superseded the Persian Empire.

We also said that these visions combine to take us through the period, referred to In Luke 21:24 as 'the times of the Gentiles' which will be concluded with the coming of the Kingdom of God in power (Daniel 2:44-45, 7:13-14). Next we will consider the fourth Kingdom which, clearly, bridges the gap between the Greek Empire and the coming of God's Kingdom.

The Fourth Kingdom Considered

The Legs of Iron & Feet of Iron and Clay (Imperialism)

The Materials, referred to in Daniel 2:40 - 42, are not precious but are strong. As was demonstrated in chapter 5, there is a reverse order of value and strength in the metals which make up the statue in the vision.

These materials (iron and iron mixed with clay) represent Rome. Iron is the metal of weapons and warfare. Rome crushed every Kingdom in its way and every rebellion fiercely through its superior military tactics and innovative and distinctive new weapon - the short stabbing sword. It was also brutal in the manner in which it defeated its enemies, for example, Carthage was utterly and systematically destroyed by the Romans in 149 BC as an act of vengeance for Hannibal's previous occupation of Italy.

Rome not only succeeded the Greek Empire but also conquered it; however, this fourth empire is not exclusively Rome since the period it spans takes us through to the establishment of God's earthly Kingdom established with the Second Coming (the image is destroyed by the crushing of the 10 toes)[17].

The vision tells us that this Kingdom is:

- Strong and ruthless (v. 40)
- It is divided into two parts (v.41). The Roman Empire divided into two parts in the fourth century AD with the western half becoming the Holy Roman Empire with its capital Rome and the

[17] *The stone referred to in Daniel 2:45 is not the church as some have suggested. The stone destroyed the Kingdoms completely and then filled the whole earth. The destiny of the church is not to destroy earthly Kingdoms but to be the agent of the Kingdom of God until King Jesus returns to destroy the Kingdoms of this world. He is the rock 'cut without hands' (Daniel 2: 45 - i.e. not man made but divinely conceived). He is 'the stone which the builders rejected...' (1 Peter 2:7). It is He who, on His return, will ultimately destroy all authorities raised up against God and His government.*

eastern half becoming the Byzantine Empire with its capital Constantinople.

- It has two materials of different strengths which do not bind well together (iron and clay). This represents the governmental form of Kingship combined with Democracy.
- There is no adherence in the materials - either one or the other form of government dominates. There is a lack of cohesiveness - authority rests with the masses.
- The 10 Toes correlate to the horns on the beast in Daniel 7 and in Revelation 13, as will be explained below.

The Indescribable Beast - Daniel 7:7 to 8

When looking upon the fourth beast in his vision, Daniel cannot come up with a description of this beast and simply refers to it as being 'dreadful and terrifying and extremely strong'. This beast has:

- 'Large iron teeth' to crush
- Ten Horns (during the vision, three are uprooted and replaced by one)
- Claws of bronze (v.19)

In Daniel 7:15-22, Daniel wants to know what this beast means. The interpretation is given in verses 23-28.

- In verse 17 we are told that it will 'arise from the earth'. This is synonymous with the sea in v.2 and stands for the Gentile nations.
- In verse 23 it is described as being 'different from all other Kingdoms'.
- Verse 23 tells us it 'will devour the whole earth'. Whilst the previous empires were given dominion over the whole earth they never took it. We are told that this Kingdom will. (Rome never did this. It didn't conquer as far east as the Greeks had done, nor did it take Scotland or the Parthian empire with which it was co-existent).
- In verse 24 we are told that ten Kingdoms will arise out of this empire. Some have suggested that this refers to the European Union, however, there were never just ten Kingdoms in the Roman Empire and there are more than ten Kingdoms in the

European Union. Rather it is safer to assume that this refers to ten world regions (since this empire will consume the whole earth) which are yet to arise. They arise out of the single conquering Kingdom (v.24).

- Verses 24 to 25 refer to the final king of this worldwide empire, the Antichrist, who will personally take control of 3 of the world regions only after the 10 world regions have arisen.
- In verse 25 we are told that this final king will rule for 3 ½ years (cf. Revelation 12:6). 'He will wage war on the saints' for this period.
- Verse 27 concludes the interpretation by affirming that this final king will ultimately be destroyed when Christ returns, at which point the government of this world will be handed over to the 'saints'[18].

The Fourth Beast in History

The Historical Development of Rome

Rome was characterised by Republican Imperialism (or monarchical democracy). It had an emperor (Caesar) and a parliament / senate. This is reflected in the iron & clay mentioned above. In this, it was different from all empires which had preceded it.

It crushed by imposing direct roman rule instead of setting up a local ruler in each of its dominions (e.g. Pontius Pilate was a Roman who was sent by Rome to govern Judea). Previous empires would rule through the existing nobles of a particular state who would give tribute to the conqueror but Rome always installed a Roman governor.

These two principles have characterised every government established since the Roman Empire including British imperialism, American republicanism and Russian communism. There is always a head of state and a parliament. These two do not mix - either one or the other is dominant.

[18] *The word 'saints' here could be taken to refer specifically and exclusively to Israel, however, due to the fact that Daniel would not have had a concept of gentiles coming into the covenant through the sacrificial death of the Messiah, it is not surprising that this generic term is used. We must assume that since this term is used in the New Testament to refer to the Church (e.g. Romans 8:27), it may or may not include the Church in this context.*

A Divided Kingdom

As mentioned above, the fact that there are two legs to this Kingdom tells us that this is a divided Kingdom. In AD 364, the Roman Empire did split into two. The west was ruled from Rome; the east from Constantinople. The development of the two halves of the old Roman Empire is summarised below.

I. Development of the Empire in the West

- In AD 479 Rome was sacked
- In AD 800, The Holy Roman Empire of the Francs was established under Charlemagne.
- In AD 962, the Germans took over the empire under Otto and established the Holy Roman Empire of the German Nation (the title 'Kaiser' is the Germanic form of 'Caesar').
- All subsequent western democracies were established along the same lines (e.g. Napoleon styled himself as 'Emperor' following the establishment of mob rule in France; Victoria became Empress, re-establishing the Roman nomenclature).
- The current centre of the western half of the empire is Washington DC, which models itself directly on the Roman form of Government, except that it uses the title 'President' instead of 'Emperor'.

II. Development in the East

- The Byzantine Empire continued intact using the Roman form of government until its defeat by the Turks.
- On the Arab invasion of Turkey in 15th Century, the leaders of the east fled to Moscow and Romanized the Russian Government (the title 'Tsar' is the Russian form of 'Caesar').
- Moscow has remained the capital of the eastern half of the empire ever since, at least until recent times.
- During the Communist years we saw Moscow exercising the Roman style hegemony over the 'conquered nations'.

THIS BRINGS US TO THE PRESENT DAY. We are still in the 2 division stage of the Roman Empire.

We have been through a time where the barriers between east and west have been broken down (the destruction of the Berlin Wall in 1989 was more than symbolic) and where there has been talk of a 'New World Order'. This paves the way towards unifying the east and west under one world government in order to 'devour the whole earth'. Following the vision through to its conclusion, we can see that from our current position of relative peace between east and west, once peace has been made with the Islamic world, and with increasing globalisation and the structures of the United Nations, it is not inconceivable that there will be a move towards a single world government with ten regionalised democracies. From this point it would not be difficult to see how, if things were to deteriorate, one ruler might arise with the mandate to bring peace and stability to the world and thus become the world's 'saviour' (the Antichrist).

The Beast of Revelation

In Revelation 13:1-7, John describes a beast very similar to the Beast of Daniel; however there is some additional information in John's revelation:

- Verse 1 tells us it has seven heads (see below for an explanation of the seven heads).
- Verse 2 describes the beast as 'like a leopard'; it has 'feet like those of a bear'; it has a 'mouth like the mouth of a lion'. These are familiar images taken from the other beasts in Daniel 7. We can see from this that it has characteristics of all of the preceding empires – swiftness, strength, and the ability to devour ferociously.
- In verse 2, we are also told that it is energised by the power of Satan – the dragon.
- Verse 3 tells us that one of its heads is slain but is still alive. The suggestion is that the Antichrist will have a counterfeit death and resurrection (cf. 13:14 and 17:8).
- In verse 5 we are told that he has authority for 42 months (i.e. 3 ½ years).
- We are told in verse 7 that he is given authority over 'every tribe and people and tongue and nation'. Once more we see the rulership of the whole earth being given to an earthly empire.

In these verses, the Antichrist becomes synonymous with the empire. It is difficult to separate one from the other – he typifies it, heads it up and seduces the whole world, but wages war on the saints – specifically Jews and Christians in this context (12:13-17).

The Seven Heads Explained in Revelation 17: 9-10

In Revelation 17:9-10, we are given an explanation of the seven heads of the beast. We are told that the seven heads are seven mountains and seven kings, five of whom have already died, one is the current one and one is yet to come. The five who have fallen cannot be Roman emperors since more than five had already preceded John's writing of Revelation. A suggested interpretation is that this refers to the five forms of government within the Roman Empire period which preceded John's writings:

i. Tarquin Kings 753 – 510 BC
ii. Counsellors 509 – 494 BC
iii. Plebeians 494 – 390 BC
iv. Republicans 390 – 59 BC
v. Triumphvirate 59 - 27BC (Julius Caesar's reign)
vi. Imperialism 27BC to the Middle of the Tribulation (Augustus Caesar onward)
vii. Antichrist Reign Middle of Tribulation to the return of Christ

This last has not yet come. He is a head and a horn and is an absolute dictator energised by Satan.

Finale - Revelation 17:14-18

The final empire under the Antichrist will be defeated by the Lamb who is Jesus because He is Lord of Lords and King of Kings. Suffice to say for the moment that this is indicated in Daniel 2:44-45, 7:26-27 and Revelation 17:14.

Summary

In this chapter, we have considered the fourth empire as portrayed in the visions of Daniel, and have shown it to be Rome, although not exclusively the historical Roman Empire, but the Roman form of government which will continue through to the return of Christ.

Chapter 7

Studies in Daniel: The Rise of Empires III

Introduction

In this chapter, we will complete our studies in Daniel. Once more, we will begin our journey in the past in order to bring us to some understanding of the future.

The Little Horn

Returning to Daniel 8:9-14, we will first consider the Little Horn arising out of one of the horns of the Ram. As mentioned above, the ram represents Greece and the little horn referred to in these verses grows up out of the four horns which have succeeded the 'conspicuous horn' (Daniel 8:5). In other words, this little horn is a king who arose out of the line of one of Alexander's generals and came to the fore in the years that followed the division of Alexander's empire.

This whole vision has to do with a king who arose from the line of Seleucus, who ruled the territories of Syria, Babylonia and the east to the Indus River. The name of this king was Antiochus Epiphanes. His name means 'the manifest God'. His quest was to take over Egypt and the battleground of the conquest was Israel. Thus, he features strongly in this vision because what he did affected 'the beautiful land'.

He reigned between 175 - 164 BC. Details of his story can be found in 1st and 2nd Maccabees (Apocrypha) or in the writings of Josephus[19].

He desecrated the Temple and stopped the rites of circumcision. He removed the treasures from the temple and set up false idols and sacrificed pigs and unclean beasts on the altars (v.11). He set up 'the Abomination of Desolation' on the altar: the statue of Jupitas Olympias (Zeus) which was erected right on the altar itself.

Many Jews took part in this and concurred with his actions. They were Helenisers who wanted the Greek culture to be adopted in Israel in place of the Mosaic Law (v.12). He flung 'truth to the ground' in that if anyone was found with the law in their possession they were killed.

According to verse 14, this period of desecration would last for '2300 evenings and mornings; then the holy place will be properly restored'. Historically, this occurred exactly as Daniel had prophesied, as follows:

- The persecution began Sept 9th 171 BC
- The 'Abomination of Desolation' was set up on Sept 9th 168 BC
- The cleansing occurred December 25th 165BC,

A TOTAL of exactly 2300 days.

Verse 17 tells us that this vision 'pertains to the time of the end'; in other words, these things have ramifications beyond Antiochus Epiphanes. Whilst this vision was literally fulfilled in the person of Antiochus Epiphanes, it will be fulfilled again at the End Times. In this sense, he is a type of the Antichrist as we will see in Chapter 11 of Daniel. In Matthew 24:15, Jesus, when speaking of the End Times, refers to this

[19] *Flavius Josephus was a Jewish historian, born four years after the crucifixion of Jesus (A.D. 37). He was the son of a priest named Matthias and a mother who descended from the royal Jewish family of the Hasmoneans. In his youth he studied the Pharisees, Sadducees and Essenes, the three main Jewish sects of his day and at the age of nineteen became a Pharisee. At the age of 27 he travelled to Rome and commenced his Romanophile tendency. On returning to Judea, he reluctantly joined the revolt which was just commencing (AD 64). Having been taken captive and consequently having ingratiated himself with Vespasian, who went on to become Emperor, he became a mediator and interpreter for the Romans, appealing to his countrymen to lay down their arms. After the war, he returned with Vespasian to Rome and remained under his patronage for the rest of his life. Thus, he wrote his histories, Jewish Antiquities and War, for a Roman audience.*

passage and confirms that the Abomination of Desolation will be set up once more in the temple in Jerusalem. Whether this will be a statue of Jupiter Olympias is doubtful, but certainly it will be the setting up of something that will defile the 'holy place'. As is stated by Matthew in this same verse, 'let the reader understand'.

In verse 19, the angelic visitor refers to a period towards the end which he calls the 'Indignation'. Again, turning to Matthew 24, we see in verse 21, Jesus referring to a period of great tribulation, which will occur during the End Times. Suffice to say that the time towards the end, just before and during the reign of the Antichrist will be a time of devastation, trouble and hardship for the world.

In verses 23 to 25 we have an interpretation of verses 9 to 14, which tells us about the nature and character, not only of Antiochus Epiphanes, but also of the Antichrist.

Looking specifically at verses 23 to 25, we are told that:

- He is 'insolent and skilled in intrigue'
- The power source is not his own: he is energised by the power of Satan (cf. Revelation 13:2).
- He will destroy in Satan's power
- He will succeed and do what he wants
- He will destroy the mighty and the holy (two thirds of the Jews alive in that day - Zechariah 13:8-9)
- He is crafty and deceitful
- He will magnify himself
- He will destroy many
- He will oppose Christ
- He will be defeated

Daniel 9

Turning over to Daniel 9, we find a further angelic revelation which again confirms the sequence of events which culminate in the rise of the Antichrist.

This passage begins with Daniel praying for the ending of the captivity of his people, having noted that Jeremiah prophesied that they would be restored after 70 years (Jeremiah 29:10), and having observed that this period was almost up. In response to his prayers, Daniel receives an angelic visitation by none other than the Archangel Gabriel. Rather than bringing him specific information concerning the restoration of Israel, he gives Daniel some additional information which relates to the End Times.

His opening declaration in chapter 9 verse 24 is that seventy 'weeks' have been 'decreed for your people' to:

i. Finish the transgression (the rejection of the Messiah - Rom 11:26)
ii. Make an end of (seal up) sin (Jesus dealt with the issue of sin once and for all)
iii. Make atonement for iniquity (through Jesus' sacrificial death)
iv. To bring in the Messianic Kingdom in everlasting righteousness
v. To seal up (or cause to cease or fulfil) the vision and prophecy
vi. To anoint the temple, the most holy place.

Gabriel is saying that all of these things must be accomplished during this period. The literal meaning of the word translated 'weeks' in the NASB[20] is 'sevens'. There is no suggestion here that this refers to seven day weeks and within the context of the passage, and other scriptures it is safer to interpret this as years. In other words, a period of 490 years have been allocated or set aside for Israel for the fulfilment of these things.

These 490 years are also split into two distinct phases:

7 x 7 years plus 62 x 7 years = 49 years plus 434 years from the issuing of the decree (see below) to the coming of the messiah

1 x 7 years = 7 years. These will occur at the end.

We are told in verse 25 that the starting point for the first 69 weeks is the 'issuing of a decree to restore and rebuild Jerusalem' and the end point is the coming of 'Messiah the Prince'. As to which decree this period commences from, we have three Options:

1. The Decree of Cyrus issued in 539 BC (66 years into the Captivity) which allowed for the first return of Jews to Jerusalem to rebuild the temple (Ezra 1:1-4).

[20] *New American Standard Bible.*

2. The order of Darius issued in 521 BC (Ezra 6:1-12) which re-confirmed the decree of Cyrus concerning the reconstruction of the temple (the fall of the temple was 586 BC; reconstruction was commenced in 521 BC and completed in 516BC).
3. Artaxerxes' decree to Nehemiah to rebuild the walls, issued in 444 BC (Nehemiah 2:1-8).

All of these are problematical in terms of 69 x 7's. We also have to make an adjustment for the fact that in the Jewish calendar, a year is a lunar year (360 days). Thus, in our calculation we have to take off five days for each year. By this means, in 483 years we lose 2415 days which is equivalent to 6.6 years.

If we take each of these in turn:

1. Commencing in 539 BC and adding 483 years, adjusting for the lunar calendar, takes us to 62 BC. This drops us short of any significant date concerning the coming of the Messiah.
2. Commencing 521 BC and adding 483 years, adjusting for the lunar calendar, takes us to 45 BC. Once more this drops us significantly short of any significant date.
3. Commencing in 444 BC and adding 483 years, adjusting for the lunar calendar, takes us to 32AD. This is approximately the time at which Jesus entered Jerusalem in triumph before being crucified.

Obviously, this last date ties in with the prophecy, however, it is debatable whether the 'decree' of Artaxerxes is really a decree or whether this is really what was prophetically intended. On the other hand, Daniel 7:25 refers to a decree 'to restore and rebuild Jerusalem'. The first two decrees above dealt only and specifically with the rebuilding of the temple. It is exclusively the latter decree which concerns the rebuilding of the walls of the city. Thus, this last decree is the most probable of the three.

Whichever view we take with regard to the above decrees, the next significant event noted in the prophecy is that 'the Messiah will be cut off and have nothing' (v.26). This is a reference to the crucifixion, resurrection and ascension of the Messiah. Whilst Israel expected the Messiah to come and establish an earthly Kingdom with Jerusalem as his headquarters, that event is reserved for the End Times. Instead, in terms of earthly power, Jesus currently has nothing, although he reigns supremely over all spiritual powers. Instead His Kingdom is in the hearts and lives of those who make Him their lord by choice. Thus his reign currently is spiritual as opposed to physical and political.

Continuing in verse 26, after the 69 sevens, and the cutting off of the Messiah we have a gap between the 69th and 70th year during which time:

- The people from whom the Antichrist will come, will 'destroy the city and sanctuary'
- The end will be with a flood
- Even until the end there will be war.

This verse tells us a number of things. Firstly, that Jerusalem and the temple will be destroyed by the Antichrist's people. This event happened circa 70AD when the Romans sacked Jerusalem and the inhabitants were scattered. If the Antichrist's people did this, this tells us that the Antichrist is of Roman extraction. We can either take this to mean that the Antichrist will be of Italian descent, or that he will be descended from one of the peoples who made up the Roman army[21]. Next the verse tells us that the remainder of history will be typified by wars, even until the end. This we know is true. Each and every century of history since that time has been marked by war and bloodshed. Finally, we are told that the end will come 'with a flood' (v.26). In prophetic language, a flood speaks of a military invasion. Thus, we can confirm that at the end there will be a military invasion of Israel (cf. Revelation 12:15-16 and also Chapter 9, which considers other Old Testament prophetic scriptures).

At this point in the prophecy, we jump to the last seven years of human history with the words 'and he' (v.27). The 'he' here refers to 'the prince who is to come': the Antichrist who will come into prominence in the final seven years of human history – the period known as the Great Tribulation. This relates to the last of our 'sevens', making up the seventieth seven.

[21] *The Roman legions which sacked Jerusalem were the Legio XII Fulminata, the Legio XV Apollinaris, the Legio V Macedonia, and the Legio X Fretensis. These were all Italian regiments, although they may have had some members from other nations amongst them.*

- In verse 27, we are told the following details about this final seven year period:
- There are two distinct phases of three and a half years per phase within the last seven years
- The start of the final seven years is when the Antichrist makes a firm covenant (with Israel). The covenant will be broken half way through the Tribulation and the sacrifices of Israel will be caused to cease (which pre-supposes that they have started by then and that the temple has been rebuilt - Rev 11:2).
- We are told that 'on the wing of abomination' (v.27), which is the pinnacle of the temple, the worship of the Antichrist will begin with the setting up of his image in the temple.
- He will make the Jews desolate (cf. Matt 24:15-22).
- This will happen until the 'complete destruction' decreed for the Antichrist is poured out.

Daniel 10

Moving on to the remainder of the prophecies contained within the book of Daniel, we find that chapters 10, 11 and 12 of Daniel are one continual thought or vision. Chapter 10 deals with the events surrounding Daniel receiving this final vision; chapter 11 is the vision in full detail; and chapter 12 contains concluding remarks concerning the vision.

In verse 1 of chapter 10 we are told that this vision was received in the 3rd Year of Cyrus (536-535 BC). At this point in the narrative, Daniel is between 84 and 85 years old. He has been mourning and fasting for three weeks during the Passover and has therefore missed the Passover celebration. The decree of Cyrus has been made (see above) but only 49,000 Jews have chosen to return to Jerusalem. They had begun to rebuild the temple but through opposition had stopped building. It is in this context in which the angelic visitor brings him 'what is inscribed in the writing of truth' (v.21) - God's pre-written plan of the world.

Daniel 11

Moving on to the actual revelation in chapter 11, in verse 2 we are told that 3 more Persian kings would arise after Cyrus, and then a fourth who would make war on Greece. This occurred historically as follows:

- Cyrus ruled the Medo-Persian Empire, including Babylon, between 539 and 530 BC.
- Cambyses, the son of Cyrus (Ahasuerus of Ezra 4:6) reigned from 530 to 522 BC. His reign ended when he committed suicide.
- Pseudo-Smerdes ruled for seven months in 522 BC. He became king after Cambyses and had his own brother Smerdes (whom he didn't trust) murdered. Pseudo-Smerdes looked like Cambyses' brother and took the throne whilst Cambyses was away conquering Egypt. When Cambyses heard about this, he could not admit to having murdered his brother so he committed suicide. The real name of Pseudo-Smerdes was Gautama (Artaxerxes of Ezra 4:7).
- Darius 1st Hystaspes reigned between 522 and 486BC. He removed Pseudo-Smerdes after hearing about the deception and intrigues (Ezra 4:34). Haggai and Zechariah prophesied during his reign. It was this Darius who first led the Persians against the Greeks and lost at the Battle of Marathon.
- Xerxes (the 4th king) reigned between 486 and 465 BC (Ahasuerus of Esther (Esther's husband)). The Persian Empire reached its fullest extent and power under his rule (v.2). In Esther 1:1-12 we see him holding a feast which lasts for 180 days which he financed personally. Verse 2 also tells us 'He will arouse the whole empire against the realm of Greece'. He spent four years amassing a huge army of (debatably) 2.5 million troops. In 480BC he launched a war against Greece. (This war included the famous Battles of Thermopylae and Salamis).

After these 4 kings mentioned in Daniel a number of other kings arose in Persia who are not mentioned:

- Artaxerxes 1st Longimanus who reigned between 465 and 425BC (Ezra, Nehemiah and Malachi all worked / prophesied during his reign).
- Darius 2nd Ochus who reigned between 423 and 404BC.
- Artaxerxes 3rd Nemon, who reigned between 404 and 359BC. His reign was characterised by continuous rebellions.
- Artaxerxes 4th Ochus who reigned between 359 and 339BC. His Prime Minister, Bagaos, murdered him and put his son on the throne.

- Arses reigned between 338 and 336BC. Bagaos also murdered Arses and put the last Persian king on the throne.
- Darius 3rd Cordomanus reigned between 336-331 BC. He murdered Bagaos but was defeated by Alexander the Great.

Verses 3 to 4 reiterate the commencement of the Greek Empire (see chapter 5 above). The next 31 verses deal with the battles between the descendants of Ptolemy and Seleucus which, whilst interesting from an historical point of view (and in verifying the incredible accuracy of this prophecy), are not relevant to our studies of the End Times. For interest, these can be found in Appendix 2. This includes verses 21 to 34 which focus on Antiochus Epiphanes (a type of the Antichrist).

In verse 35 the focus of the passage goes through a transition, from Antiochus Epiphanes, to the Antichrist. The key here is the phrase 'until the end time; because it is still to come to the appointed time'. In other words, what has just been described concerning Antiochus Epiphanes is similar to what will happen at the end but the events of the End Times are in the future and still to come. The persecution of the Jews will happen again in a similar manner in the future. All that has gone before was literally fulfilled. All that is detailed from this point forward is yet to be fulfilled.

Verses 36 to 45 describe the actions and character of the Antichrist as follows:

- In verse 36 we see the self-exaltation and rise of the Antichrist. 'He will magnify himself above every god'. In other words, he will claim deity for himself (cf. 2 Thessalonians 2:3-4, Rev 13:1-8). The word 'Indignation' here refers to the time of tribulation at the end (cf. Matthew 24:21).
- Verse 37 tells us 'He will have no regard for the gods of his fathers' i.e. pagan gods. He will have no regard for the 'desire of women' – either that which women desire (the Tammus cult was particularly popular among women at that time), or the desire for women – he will not desire the love of women which is natural to men. He will not regard any gods or men or women but only himself.
- Instead, verse 38 tells us, he will worship 'the god of fortresses' – he will honour power and might. The text adds 'a god whom his

fathers did not know' i.e. Satan.

- Verse 39 tells us that he is energised by Satan (2 Thessalonians 2:8-10. Rev 13:1-8). He will reward all who help him with money and position and will divide up the conquered territory for the price of loyalty.
- Verse 40 describes the wars of the End Times. In the book of Revelation, there are three World Wars mentioned as occurring during the Tribulation:
    - The first one is in Revelation 6 which happens at the beginning of the Tribulation
    - The second one is in the middle of Tribulation
    - The third one is at the end of Tribulation and is widely known as Armageddon.

  This passage deals with the middle one.
- Verse 40 also mentions a number of kings: the King of the South is Egypt; the King of the North is Syria
- The term 'He will enter...' in verse 41 means he will invade and defeat Egypt and Syria. He will also enter Israel (Rev 11:2). Verse 41 tells us that Edom, Moab and Ammon avoid his domination (modern day Jordan). These are the places where the people of Israel will flee during this time, as indicated in Matthew 24:15-22 (See Rev 12:6 &13-14).
- Verses 42 to 43 describe the fall of Egypt, Libya and Ethiopia.
- The 'East and North' of verse 44 are Syria and Iraq. He will go forth and destroy them both.
- Verse 45 tells us he will set up his headquarters in Jerusalem (Rev 11:1-2). He can then commit 'the abomination of desolation'. The words, 'he will come to his end...' tell us that he will be killed in the conflict.

Daniel 12

Moving on to the closing remarks of the prophecy, and indeed of the book of Daniel, we see that Verse 1 of chapter 12 correlates directly with Revelation 12:7-9. In these verses we see the end time struggle between Michael, the Archangel assigned to watch over Israel (cf. Daniel 10:13 & 21), who takes up the battle against Satan, on behalf of the Jewish people. This will be a time of the greatest persecution of the Jews ever (v.1). However, those whose names are written in the Lamb's book of

Life will be delivered (see Matthew 24:22 (cf. Zechariah 13:8-9 which indicates that only one third of the Jews will survive this period)).

Verses 2 to 3 tell us of the resurrection after the time of Tribulation. There are two resurrections here: one to 'everlasting life' and one to 'everlasting contempt' (cf. Revelation 20:5, 12-15, Isaiah 24:21-22). We will deal with the resurrections in Chapter 15.

Verse 4 correlates directly with Revelation 22:10. Daniel is instructed to seal up his book because it is for a future time. John is told not to seal up his book because it is for the present era which will culminate in these events. The books of Daniel and Revelation will bring the 'increase of knowledge' concerning these things.

In verses 5 to 7, two additional Angelic beings appear to act as witnesses. The angel swears that the final period of the Tribulation will last for three and a half years. The purpose of the period is to shatter the power of Israel, and when they are facing annihilation the time will be completed.

In verses 8 to 10 Daniel asks for clarification but does not receive it.

Verse 11 tells us that the abomination of desolation is set up for 1290 days (30 days after the end of the Tribulation). An additional 45 days beyond the 1290 (75 days beyond the 1260 days) are mentioned in verse 12. Therefore, there is a period of 75 days between the end of the Tribulation and the setting up of the millennial Kingdom[22]. The purpose of the 75 day interval is to make the world ready for the Kingdom including the first resurrection and the removal of the 'Abomination of Desolation'.

Summary

In this chapter we have concluded our studies in Daniel and in so doing have learned much about the nature of the Antichrist and the time of his rule. We have seen that Antiochus Epiphanes was a type of the Antichrist and in the time of his rule over the land of Israel, we see much that will be repeated by the Antichrist during the End Times.

---

[22] *This is subject to the millennial view taken by the reader – see chapter 3.*

Chapter 8

Studies in Zechariah

Introduction

Like Daniel, Zechariah is different to most of the other prophetic books of the Old Testament in that it was written in the post-exilic period of Israel's history, as also were Haggai and Malachi. Whereas the other prophetic books spoke into the disobedience of Israel with proclamations of judgements and promises of restoration, the prophecies of this book were given during a time of restoration. The message of the other post-exilic books, Haggai and Malachi, was declared to stir the people out of complacency and into righteous action. Zechariah, on the other hand begins with a call to repentance given to the returned exiles, but very soon moves into a set of visions and prophetic scriptures that look far beyond the immediate times during which the prophet spoke.

The Visions of the Book of Zechariah

In chapters 1 to 6 of Zechariah we have a series of eight visions. We may see these as eight parts of one vision, however, whichever way we choose to view them, there are eight distinct parts to what Zechariah sees. Since in scripture eight is the number of new beginnings, it is not surprising that these eight visions occur in Zechariah which was given at a time of new beginning (restoration) for the people of Israel.

The visions are as follows:

1. The rider amongst the myrtle trees (1:7-17)
2. Four horns and four craftsmen (1:18-21)
3. A man with a measuring line (2:1-13)
4. Clean garments for Joshua, the High Priest (3:1-10)
5. The gold lampstand and the two olive trees (4:1-14)
6. The flying scroll (5:1-5)
7. The woman in the basket (5:5-11)
8. The four chariots (6:1-10)

We will take each of these visions in turn and attempt to interpret them particularly as they give insight into the End Times.

Vision 1: The Rider amongst the Myrtle Trees

In this vision (Zechariah 1:7-17) the prophet sees a set of riders standing amongst some myrtle trees. Like Daniel, he has an angelic interpreter made available to him to help him understand what he is seeing. It is confirmed to him by one of the riders that they are 'those whom the Lord has sent to patrol the earth' and that in so doing they have found that all is 'peaceful and quiet'. The image of riders being sent forth to inspect the world would have been familiar to those of Zechariah's day since the Persian monarchs used such riders to patrol their empires and to bring back news of its condition. To any whom they passed, they were a reminder of the overlords who ruled them. In this instance, the riders are servants of the king of all the earth and remind us that, ultimately, God is in command of all.

Elsewhere in scripture, myrtle trees are associated with the restoration of Israel (see Isaiah 44:19 and 55:13). Thus we have a picture of the earth, following the restoration of Israel to the land, in which the earth is at peace and therefore the angel of the Lord (the rider whom Zechariah first saw) asks how long the Lord will have no compassion on Jerusalem. In other words, the angel is asking God for justice since it appears that the nations who exacted the exile upon Israel and who destroyed Jerusalem have escaped without being punished themselves.

The Lord responds by stating the following:

- He is jealous for Jerusalem (v.14)
- He is angry with the nations who took his judgement further than he had given them scope so to do (v.15).
- He will restore Jerusalem and cause it to prosper once more and ensure the temple is rebuilt (v.16-17).

The message given to Zechariah is that despite the apparent injustice that currently prevails, ultimately, God will bring about justice for Israel and upon those errant nations.

In Zechariah's time the temple was rebuilt, however, the restoration prefigured here is concurrent with the judgement of the nations. Thus, this passage is referring beyond the immediacy of Zechariah's time to the End Time restoration of Israel and the judgement of the nations, to be meted out at the return of the Messiah.

Vision 2: Four Horns and Four Craftsmen

In this vision (Zechariah 1:18-21), the prophet first sees four horns which are identified by his angelic interpreter as those who 'scattered Judah, Israel, and Jerusalem', i.e. those nations, and particularly the kings of those nations, who were responsible for the scattering. Despite the recent restoration of some Jews to the land to rebuild the temple, in Zechariah's day much of the nation was still resident in the places where they had been taken into exile.

In response to the horns, Zechariah sees four craftsmen who came 'to terrify them, to throw down the horns of the nations who have lifted up their horns against the land of Judah to scatter it'. At first view, this seems quite bizarre: how can mere craftsmen (carpenters and the like) terrorise the rulers of nations. The answer is that it is craftsmen who will rebuild the temple of the Lord. This same Hebrew word (harasim) is used often in the Old Testament scriptures (see, Exodus 28:11, 2 Kings 12:11, 1 Chronicles 22:15, 29:5, 2 Chronicles 24:12, 2 Kings 22:6, 2 Chronicles 34:11) in association with those who would work on the house of the Lord. In other words, Zechariah is seeing that during his time, it is not the direct intervention of God which will reverse the scattering of the people of God, but the rebuilding of the temple which will draw the nation back to Himself.

Ultimately, it is the completion of the building of the spiritual house of God, which will be the backdrop for the final judgement of the nations at the return of the Messiah.

Vision 3: A Man with a Measuring Line

The third vision (Zechariah 2:1-5) is followed immediately by three prophetic words (v.6-13) which confirm and add to the vision. Essentially, the vision Zechariah sees is of a man with a measuring rod in his hand going out to measure Jerusalem presumably, from what follows, with a view to rebuilding the walls. The angelic interpreter is instructed by another angel to stop the man since God 'will be a fire around her' and 'will be the glory in her midst'.

In chapter 1 verse 16, the Lord has already declared that 'a measuring line will be stretched out over Jerusalem' and therefore we can assume that in his zeal this man is seeking to carry out the word of the Lord, however, his timing is wrong (the walls were not rebuilt for another 75 years when God raised up Nehemiah to do the work). The Lord declares that he will protect Jerusalem whilst the work of rebuilding the temple is progressing.

The oracles that follow instruct the people of God to flee from the places where they have been scattered, from 'the land of the north (Assyria) and from Babylon (v.6), because his judgement will come upon those lands (v.9). The context, and the words that follow show that this goes beyond Zechariah's day and into God's End Time purposes since he declares that he will live in the midst of them. This reflects the return of the Messiah to rule from Jerusalem. It also reflects the union of Israel and the New Covenant people of God in the End Times as it declares that 'many nations will join themselves to the Lord in that day and will become my people'.

Finally, the last oracle also declares (v.12) that the Lord will again choose Jerusalem. This is a repetition of 1:17 and gives us the timing of when the events recorded in this verse will occur – at the return of Christ. This ties up with other prophetic passages such as Isaiah 2:2-4.

Vision 4: Clean Garments for Joshua, the High Priest

In the fourth vision (3:1-10), Zechariah sees Joshua, the High Priest, standing before the Lord with Satan 'at his right hand to accuse him'. He is dressed in 'filthy garments' which clearly represent his uncleanness and unfitness to serve as High Priest, however, the Lord himself commands that his uncleanness is taken away and replaced with suitable robes (v.4). Zechariah speaks up and requests that Joshua's turban is also replaced, which is done. Joshua is then instructed by the Lord to walk in obedience and then his reward will be 'free access' into God's presence.

We are then told in verse 8 that Joshua and his friends (presumably the other priests) are a symbol of the truth which will be demonstrated in 'the Branch'. The Branch is a term used several times in the Old Testament to indicate the Messiah (see Psalm 80:15, Isaiah 4:2, Isaiah 11:1, Jeremiah 23:5, Jeremiah 33:15). Thus, Joshua and his friends are symbols of the Messiah in his priesthood, however, it is he who will 'remove the iniquity of that land in one day' (v.9). That is exactly what Jesus did in his sacrificial death on the cross and has thereby opened up a future of peace where 'everyone of you will invite his neighbour to sit under his vine and under his fig tree' (v.10) which will be fulfilled in his Messianic Kingdom. This single day could also prefigure the redemption of Israel 'in that day' prefigured in Zechariah 13 (see below).

Vision 5: The Gold Lampstand and the Two Olive Trees

In the fifth vision (4:1-14), after Zechariah has been roused from his sleep by the angel, he sees a golden lampstand[23] with seven spouts with two olive trees nearby on either side of it. In contrast with the lampstand described in Exodus 25, the lampstand in this passage has a bowl at the top. Webb speculates that this bowl contained oil and from it oil flowed to the seven lamps[24]. From verse 12 we also know that the two olive trees pour oil from themselves and this feeds the lampstand. In observing these, he asks his angelic interpreter what the objects are i.e. what their meaning is. The remainder of the passage is a

---

[23] *For a description of the lampstand in more detail and its use in the tabernacle, see Exodus 25:31-40 and Leviticus 24:1-4. Also, note that in Solomon's temple (1 Kings 7:49), ten such lampstands were used to give light in the Holy Place, but in this rebuilt temple only one is used (see 1 Maccabees 1:21).*

[24] *Webb, The Message of Zechariah p.91*

conversation between the angel and Zechariah which defines the items.

In verse 4, Zechariah asks the angel to interpret what he is seeing. The angel expresses surprise that Zechariah doesn't already know the meaning and then goes on to explain that the vision is a symbolic representation of the word of the Lord to Zerubbabel, the governor who was responsible for the work of rebuilding the temple. The word is threefold:

- Zerubbabel will complete the work, not in his own strength but by the anointing and enabling of the Holy Spirit (v.6).
- Zerubbabel will clear every obstacle out of the way which currently stands against the achievement of the completion of the temple (v.7).
- Zerubbabel will preside over the ceremonial fitting of the capstone, the stone that will complete the building (v.7).
- Zerubbabel has already laid the foundation stone of the temple and will finish the work (v.9). When this happens, this will confirm that Zechariah has indeed received the word of the Lord.

The lampstand itself is reminiscent of Revelation chapter 1 where we see the sevenfold lampstand as representative of seven churches. In Zechariah, the lampstand represents God's people who are fulfilling His work of rebuilding the temple and will complete this work through the power of the Holy Spirit ('"Not by might, nor by power but by my Spirit'" says the lord' (v.6)).

The concluding remark by the angel concerning the seven eyes of the Lord which 'rove to and fro throughout the earth' (v.10) takes us back to the riders in chapter 1 and there is confirmation again that the rebuilding of the temple is a crucial step towards God bringing judgement on those nations who have been vindictive towards Israel (see Vision 2 above).

Zechariah questions further concerning the meaning of the olive trees and the angel gives supplementary information concerning these (v.11-14) and declares that they are 'the two anointed ones who are standing by the Lord of the whole earth' (v.14). Whilst many have speculated as to whom these two might be, the obvious answer in the context of the passage is that these represent Joshua the High Priest and Zerubbabel the Governor - God's anointed and Spirit-filled leadership for the work of rebuilding the temple. Their anointing is feeding into the community as a whole and it is through the anointing on their leadership that the work on the temple will be completed.

In the days of the two witnesses in Revelation 11 of which Joshua and Zerubbabel are types, the spiritual house of God will be completed, as the full number of the church comes to completion just prior to the return of Christ. At that time, the witnesses will be raised up on the earth to 'prophesy for twelve hundred and sixty days'. Drawing from Zechariah it is clear that these two witnesses will also represent spiritual and political authority, anointed by the Spirit of God which will challenge the government of the Antichrist in the last three and a half years of his reign (see Revelation 11:4).

Vision 6: The Flying Scroll

In the sixth vision (5:4), Zechariah sees a flying scroll fifteen feet wide and thirty feet long with writing on both sides, which, he is informed, is a curse that will come upon everyone who steals or swears resulting in their being 'purged away', which can infer either banishment or death.

Essentially The Lord is making clear to Zechariah his intention to cleanse the land of those who violate their neighbours property or person through theft or lies. These things are counted as serious because if left untouched they would undermine the fabric of an already shaky community that must remain united to complete the work of the Lord – the rebuilding of the temple.

Vision 7: The Woman in the Basket

In the seventh vision (5:5-11), he sees a women inside an ephah[25] with a lead weight over its opening. Whilst he is watching, two winged women appear and carry the ephah with the woman inside it to Babylon where a house is built so that the woman can be 'set there on her own pedestal'.

He is told that the ephah with the woman inside it represents 'the iniquity of the people throughout the land'[26]. The use of the ephah,

---

[25] *An ephah was a container which grain was put in to be measured. Unger (p.721) defines it as 'a measure of Egyptian origin, and in very common use among Hebrews'. It was equivalent to approximately 72 pints.*

[26] *Verse 6 NIV translation.*

which was normally used to measure wheat, suggests a connection with trade. Thus, we can infer that this image represents corrupt trading practices, which need to be removed in order to cleanse the land, since these are also unrighteous practices, which undermine the unity of the people.

It is of little surprise that the item which represents corrupt commercial practice is taken to the place which represents the glory of man - Babylon. There a house is built for it - literally a temple - where it can be worshipped.

In this vision the work of God's Kingdom (the building of the temple for the glory of God) is being contrasted with the work of Man's Kingdom (the building of corrupt trading empires to the glory of Man in defiance of God). God's purpose is to remove the world's corrupt practices from amongst His people to ensure their righteousness and unity to complete the work.

The woman in this vision foreshadows 'the mother of harlots and of the abominations of the earth' who is Babylon the Great in Revelation 17 and 18. Clearly in those passages, her fall is associated with the fall of the world trading system (see Revelation 18:11-20). The suggestion is that towards the end, prior to the return of Christ, the world economic system will fall apart. It will clearly have been one of the tools of control used by the Antichrist (see Revelation 13:17), but will collapse. The Messianic Kingdom will not be dependent upon corrupt trade to sustain itself, but on the blessing of God upon crops etc. as a consequence of obedience (see Zechariah 14:17).

Vision 8: The Four Chariots.

In the eighth vision (6:1-8), Zechariah sees two bronze mountains with four chariots coming towards him from between the mountains. The horses drawing the chariots are red, black, white and dappled respectively, and they head off towards the four points of the compass. The angelic interpreter describes these chariots as 'the four spirits of heaven, going forth after standing before the Lord of all the earth' (v.5), which indicates that these riders are going out from the presence of God, having received some instruction, that they are about to carry out in accordance with the command of God.

In verse 7 we have a reference back to chapter 1 verse 11 where messengers went out to patrol the earth. It would appear that these chariots are being sent forth in response to the report given by 'the strong ones' (v.7). The outcome of the chariots going forth is that God's wrath is appeased, or literally, he is brought to 'rest' having accomplished his purpose, similar to the seventh day of creation.

In order to appreciate the meaning of this vision we need to understand the symbolism a little more. The two mountains are described as being 'bronze' which nearly always speaks of judgement in scripture (cf. for example, Exodus 27:1-8). The reference to the 'bronze mountains' here suggests that the chariots are going forth to carry out God's judgement. This, again, is confirmed in verse 8 where we see God's wrath being 'appeased'.

Some[27] have speculated that the four chariots tie up with the four empires which were to arise in the earth, detailed in Daniel (see above) since those empires did lie in the direction of the four compass points. It is clear, however, that the four chariots are emissaries of God's judgement on the nations of the whole earth. They may even correlate with the four horsemen of the apocalypse, which are also emissaries of God's judgement and whose colourings are substantively the same as the horses of these four chariots. Either way, it is safe to assume that this passage speaks of God's End Time judgement of the nations which will bring the justice for the people of Israel and for Jerusalem requested in chapter 1:12-15. Thus the vision is brought full circle.

Summary of the Visions

The visions, taken together, form a composite message which God wanted to bring to the people of Zechariah's day. This message affected both their own immediate circumstances, and also gave some details of how God would ultimately fulfill his purposes, as declared to his people, including completing his house and vindicating his people.

In summary, the keys to these visions are:

- God is jealous for his people and for Jerusalem.
- He will ensure the building of the temple by the working of His spirit through His anointed leaders.
- He will bring about the cleansing of his people and banish lying, stealing and corrupt trade practices.

[27] *E.g. Adam Clarke (see Clarke), and John Calvin (see Collins).*

- He will bring about the judgement on the nations and vindicate Israel.
- His Messiah will come and set up His Kingdom on earth.

There is also symmetry in the visions as shown below:

1	2 &3	4 & 5	6 & 7	8
Judgement of the nations anticipated	The temple to be rebuilt for righteousness	Leaders selected, cleansed, and anointed	Wickedness removed to a temple built for it in Babylon	The nations judged

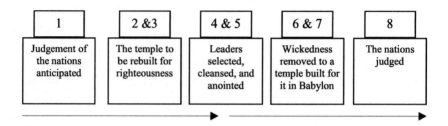

The Symbolic Crowning of Joshua the High Priest

The first half of Zechariah concludes with Zechariah being instructed by the Lord to carry out a symbolic act. He is told to take silver and gold from some who have just returned from Babylon, presumably bearing gifts for the work, and make a crown or crowns of it. He is then to crown Joshua the High Priest and to prophesy over him. Zechariah is obedient, but the prophecy he gives concerns 'the branch' which is a term that we know is a code word for the Messiah. Thus, Zechariah once more confirms that Joshua is a type of Jeshua, who will come and bear the offices of priest and king in his single personage. He will build the temple – the temple made of living stones - and He will rule.

Zechariah instructs that the crown be placed in the temple, currently being built, as a 'memorial', i.e. a reminder to all people that the Messiah will come and fulfil this word. In this way, Zechariah concludes the first section with a continual reminder that ultimately the purposes of God concerning Jerusalem, Israel and the New Covenant people will be summed up in the coming of the Messiah.

Zechariah 7 to 8

In chapters 7 to 8 of Zechariah we have an interim section prior to the commencement of the prophetic oracles which take us to the end of the book. In these chapters we see Zechariah receiving a number of specific words for the people of Israel that he delivers in a prosaic rather than oracular form. These words act as an introduction to the prophetic oracles that follow.

In chapter 7, some people arrive from Bethel to 'seek the favour of the Lord' and to ask specifically if they can stop observing the fasts which were instituted when Jerusalem was sacked. This causes Zechariah to prophesy and to call the people as a whole to repentance, reminding them that it was due to previous disobedience that the people were driven from the land. He points out that their observance of fasting has been no different from that of those against whom Isaiah prophesied in Isaiah 58, but that true fasting is accompanied with justice, kindness and compassion, not oppression and evil.

Having called the people to repentance, in chapter 8 Zechariah moves on to a promise of peace, prosperity and restoration for Jerusalem. This chapter is in two parts: verses 1 to 19 relate to the immediate future of Jerusalem and verses 20 to 23 relate to a time further off. The contrast is shown by the phrase 'in these days' used in verse 15 and 'in those days' used in verse 23.

In verses 1 to 19, the prophet proclaims that the Lord 'will return to Zion and dwell in the midst of Jerusalem'. The literal translation of this is that the Lord 'has' returned. Thus, the fulfilment of these words is associated with the completion of the temple (v.9), the place in which the Lord will dwell. Zechariah goes on to speak about a time of peace (v.4-5) and a further re-gathering of the scattered people of Israel (v.7-8). The Lord declares that he 'will cause the remnant of this people to inherit all these things' i.e. peace and prosperity, because the purpose of the Lord is 'to do good to Jerusalem...in these days' (v.15).

Whilst these promises through Zechariah were for immediate fulfilment, they also foreshadow the condition of Jerusalem following the return of the Messiah, as detailed in the other prophetic books (see Chapter 9).

The final section of this chapter concerns the future. Dispensationalists[28] position the fulfilment of these verses as either between the rapture of the church and the return of Christ – the period during which, they say, the nation of Israel will act as God's evangelists on earth; or they are

[28] *See Section 1*

positioned as being fulfilled in the Messianic Kingdom itself when Jerusalem will be the physical place from which the Messiah will rule the earth.

Alternatively, we can see these verses fulfilled in the Church age[29]: it was to Jewish believers that the Messiah revealed himself; it was upon Jewish believers that the Spirit was poured out at Pentecost; and it was from that time that Jews became the evangelists of the world, causing Gentiles from all nations to 'grasp the garment of a Jew' in order to receive the revelation of salvation and blessing which had come to the world through the Jews and from their Jewish Messiah.

Zechariah 9 to 14 – The Prophetic Oracles

In chapters 9 to 14 of Zechariah we have a series of prophetic oracles which Zechariah delivered to the people of his day. These are not dated, as the previous visions and prophesies had been, and all concern a future time, as opposed to the time of the rebuilding of the temple.

These passages are in two oracles: the first one commences in chapter 9 and goes through to chapter 11; the second one commences in chapter 12 and concludes in chapter 14. The theme of these oracles is the coming of the king. In Zechariah chapter 9, we see the first arrival of the king into Jerusalem and in chapter 14 we see the Lord as king over all. In between these depictions, we have a series of dramas presented, which show us some of the events which will take place during the End Times.

The First Oracle

In verses 1 to 8 of chapter 9 the word of the Lord 'against' Israel's immediate neighbours to the north and the west is proclaimed. Essentially, this summarises God's judgement against some of those closest to Israel who had capitalised on Israel's demise. As detailed in the next chapter, all of these nations had already suffered some judgement by the time of Zechariah's writing. However, clearly more was to come so that the end result would be that these nations would no longer gain from Israel's loss.

This passage concludes (v.8) with the promise that God, himself, will 'camp around' his house 'and no oppressor will pass over them anymore'. In other words, this prophecy looks forward to a time when

[29] *See Webb The Message of Zechariah p.125-6*

Israel will no longer be a buffer state for any passing army. Instead, the remnants of the oppressors will become incorporated into Israel just as the Jebusites were at the time of the conquest of the land (see Joshua 15:63).

In verses 9 and 10 of chapter 9 we see the coming of the king to Jerusalem. Clearly, this is the Messiah, who, in his coming, fulfils the earlier promises of 3:8 and 6:11-15. The confirmation that these verses deal with the coming of the Messiah is also given in the New Testament in Matthew 21:5 where the writer cites this passage to confirm the prophetic significance of Jesus' entry into Jerusalem.

In verse 10, we see something of the mission of the Messiah: to remove the weapons of war from Israel and to 'speak peace to the nations' as he reigns over an area that encompasses the whole world. We can interpret this in one of two ways[30]: either this is an example of prophetic foreshortening where the first coming is juxtaposed with the outcome of the second coming (the reign of the Messiah over all the earth) or we can take it that Christ now reigns over all the earth and that his mission is to bring peace to the nations – peace with God. It is certainly true that all things are subjected to Him now (Ephesians 1:22) and in that sense this prophecy has already been fulfilled, however, on His return His enemies will be made His 'footstool' (Hebrews 1:13, 10:13).

The 'peace' here promised on the coming of the Messiah is 'shalom' peace which means 'wholeness and well-being'. This is only available through the presence of Jesus with us. Webb (p. 133) in 'The Message of Zechariah', concludes his review of these verses as follows:

The coming of Jesus the Messiah was the coming of God Himself, not (at that time) to overthrow his enemies, but to proclaim peace, to offer amnesty. And He came first and foremost to Israel, his own Covenant people. He came to Jerusalem, as Zechariah had said he would, riding on a donkey. He came to God's house (the temple), and treated it as his own. The tragedy is that, when he came, his own people did not recognise him as their king. They did not know the day of God's coming to them, and ended up crucifying him. This tragedy, dark and terrible though it was, was within the plan and purpose of God to bring salvation, not just to Israel, but to the whole world. Not all rejected him, and around that crucified king, gathered a new people of God who are

[30] *Interpretation of this verse is dependent on the millennial view taken by the reader (see Section 1)*

destined to herald the good news of his Kingdom to the ends of the earth. God's Kingdom had drawn near. The end of the world had begun to happen.

In verses 11 to 17 of chapter 9, the final victory of the Messiah is foreseen but particularly from the perspective of Israel. The passage starts with the words 'as for you' referring to those who are associated with him because of the blood covenant with them. The Lord goes on to declare the restoration of 'double' to them and his use of them 'as my bow' (v.13) in 'saving them in that day' (v.16). It is clear that following this 'day' will come a time of peace and prosperity upon the land and its inhabitants.

These themes are picked up again in Zechariah chapter 10. In this chapter we have the restoration of Israel to the land, ('I will whistle for them to gather them together for I have redeemed them', v.8, see also v.6, 9-10), and also his use of them to go against his / their enemies (v.3-5). As part of the re-gathering, the enemies will be defeated (v.11). It is declared that much of the situation Israel finds itself in is because of poor shepherding (v.2-3) which causes his anger to rise but which results in him bringing about the restoration and salvation of his people himself.

In Zechariah chapter 11, the theme of the shepherding of God's people is picked up once again. In this chapter, we see that the shepherd's 'glory is ruined' (v.3), in other words, all that the leaders have been leading is destroyed. There then follows two parables acted out by Zechariah which summarise God's dealing with his people. In the first of these parables, Zechariah shepherds the 'flock doomed to slaughter' (v.4). In doing so, he destroys three other shepherds. He also takes two staffs which are named 'favour' and 'Union'. It would appear that in this parable, Zechariah is playing the part of God himself who was a shepherd to his people and blessed them and united them with himself and with each other. However, in the parable, Zechariah becomes 'impatient' (v.8) with the flock just as the flock becomes 'weary' of him, and he stops shepherding them, giving them over to destruction. In doing so he breaks the staff named favour. This is representative of God's actions with the people, of giving them over to destruction at the time of the exile, and of removing from them his favour and breaking of the covenant he had made with them (v.10). Their ultimate rejection of him as their shepherd came in the rejection of Jesus as the Messiah and his shepherding was finally valued at 30 pieces of silver (v.12 cf. Matthew 26:15). Zechariah then takes the second staff and cuts it in pieces to symbolise the dissolution of the house of Israel. This followed the crucifixion of the Messiah and occurred in the form of the Diaspora of AD 70 onwards.

In the second parable, Zechariah is instructed to play the part of a foolish shepherd (v.15). It would appear that this is not one particular leader or king but symbolises all who have led Israel for their own gain (v.16). Such Kings are blinded from seeing the state of the flock and powerless to protect them (v.17).

Together, these parables show that God's desire to shepherd his people has been rejected and the consequence of such rejection will always result in foolish shepherds being raised up and in the people being handed over to the oppressors. This has already been demonstrated in Israel's history and continued to be the case following Zechariah's day, through the inter-testamental period, when Israel was the buffer zone for the wars between the Ptolemaic and Seleucian dynasties, right through to the dispersion of AD 70 onwards. The hope for Israel in this respect is their ultimate acceptance of their Messiah and this has already been promised in chapters 9 and 10.

The Second Oracle

The second oracle is contained in chapters 12 to 14.

At the start of chapter 12 we jump straight away to the End Times with the nations surrounding Jerusalem and with God using Jerusalem as 'a cup that causes reeling' (or stagger as though drunk). We are told that 'all the nations of the earth will be gathered against it' (v.3), but God will fight on Israel's behalf (v.4), and ultimately will 'set about to destroy all the nations that come against Jerusalem' (v.9).

In verse 10, we see the repentance of the people of Israel as they look upon Jesus 'whom they have pierced' (the piercing suggested here is a stabbing which is a death blow) as he comes as their king to deliver them. They will not only recognise that he has previously been pierced but that they were the ones responsible for it. It is at this point that they will acknowledge him and 'mourn...as one mourns for an only son'. What is described here is the mourning and contrition of the whole nation, individually and collectively (v.11-14). In Revelation 1:7, this recognition and mourning is extended to 'all the tribes of the earth' and therefore whilst this restoration is specific of Israel it does not include Israel exclusively.

In chapter 13 we move from mourning to cleansing as God, himself, opens up a fountain for the inhabitants of the land to come 'for sin and for impurity' (v.1). The consequence of the mourning is that the grace of God is poured out upon his people and this results in repentance leading to a cleansing of the land from idols, false prophets (v.2-6) and 'the unclean spirit from the land' (v.3).

Chapter 13 concludes with a short poem in which God's shepherd is struck and his sheep scattered (Verse 7). Jesus himself declared in Matthew 26:13 that the fulfilment of this scripture was in his own death on the cross which resulted in his disciples being scattered, however, the consequence of his death (his rejection by his people) was the dispersion of the whole of Israel and that is also prefigured here. The poem then jumps to the final day with which chapter 12 began and declares that at that time, the time of the last battle against the nations, two thirds of Israel will 'perish' (v.8) and the remaining third will be refined 'through the fire'. It is at that point that they will call on his name and be delivered, redeemed and restored to relationship with God saying, 'the Lord is My God' (v.9).

This brings us to chapter 14 which is in two parts. The first part (verses 1 to 8) gives us a very clear picture of the events which will unfold on the day the Lord returns to Jerusalem as its Messiah and Saviour. In verses 9 to 21, Zechariah opens up something of the world as it will be during the reign of the Messiah on earth.

The events leading up to the coming of the Lord portray a time of great struggle for the people of Israel, and particularly for those living in Jerusalem at that time. We are told in verse 2 that 'the nations will be gathered' against Jerusalem. This is a reiteration of 12:2-3. We are also told that the city will be taken and half of the inhabitants exiled (v.2). It is at this point, when Israel appears to be on the point of capitulation, that 'the Lord will go forth and fight against those nations' (v.3) He will come to the Mount of Olives (c.f. Acts 1:11) and as he stands on it, it will be split in two creating a valley of escape for the remaining inhabitants of the city (v.5-6). At this point we are told that with his coming he will have 'the holy ones with him'. This is confirmed in 1 Thessalonians

4:14: 'even so, God will bring with him those who have fallen asleep in Jesus'. Also, we see that the natural order of light during the day and darkness at night will be dispensed with on that day (v.7). It appears they will not be necessary. In addition, 'living waters' will flow out from Jerusalem to the east and to the west and their flow will not change with the seasons.

In verses 9 to 21, Zechariah opens up various aspects of the post-second coming world. He starts by stating that 'the Lord will be king over all the earth' (v.9). At this point we reach the climax of human history when the rulership of the world, which was originally given to man who, through his sin, passed it on to Satan, is returned into the hands of God. The history of the world from beginning to end has come full circle and at that time God, in the form of a man, will reign over all the earth. Clearly this is associated with some geographical re-alignment (v.10) but the result of this is that Jerusalem will 'dwell in security'.

In verses 12 to 15 we see the consequences for those nations who have fought against Jerusalem. Essentially, they will be subject to an awful plague which will also affect their livestock and the result will be that Israel will plunder their riches (v.14).

In verse 16, the scene changes to dealing with the remnant of the nations who will be required, with the people of God, to come up to Jerusalem annually to celebrate the Feast of Tabernacles. This feast was a celebration of God's goodness at the time of harvest, commemorating the people of Israel's journey in tents through the wilderness. It is fitting that, during this time, the world is still called to celebrate God's goodness and provision and the completion of the journey into the Kingdom of God. However, it is clear that whilst this celebration is expected, the people's of the earth are not coerced into celebrating it, although the consequences of them not doing so are the removal of God's blessing from their lands and a plague that will come upon them. This tells us that the world in this period will not be perfect and that the nations may still be rebellious, however, the consequences of such rebellion will be direct and tangible, since the Lord himself will be present on the earth.

The chapter, and the book, conclude by affirming that just about everything in Israel, including the cooking pots, will be declared 'HOLY TO THE LORD'.

Summary

This book is specifically about God's dealings with Israel; however, since it was written in the post-exilic period, long after most of the other books of the Old Testament, its prophecies are largely centred on the coming of the Messiah, both in his incarnation, and in his glorious return.

Much of the book deals with the fact that this coming will be a key point of salvation for Israel and a final point of judgement upon the nations. However, the conclusion of this will be the reigning of the Messiah over Jew and Gentile alike, with all participating in the worship of God and in the covenant blessings of obedience.

Chapter 9

Other Old Testament References to the End Times

Introduction

There are many Old Testament passages which contain references to the End Times. Many of these deal with the judgement of the nations, but some, also deal with either the Millennium or the new heavens and the new earth. The majority of these references occur in the prophetic books.

In this section, we will examine those passages which bring the most revelation concerning the End Times. However, before delving into these scriptures, it is worth reiterating that the Old Testament contains no explicit reference to the Church. Why is this significant? Because if we base our understanding of the End Times and the patterns of events that unfold exclusively on the Old Testament scriptures, and without reference to the clear teaching given by Jesus in Matthew 24, we will assume that the Church has no part to play in the End Times. This has led some to adopt a pre-tribulation rapture position (see Chapter 1 for a discussion on the relationship between Israel and the Church as it relates to the End Times and Chapter 3 for a discussion of the various options concerning the rapture.).

With this in mind, our starting point is to say that, whilst these scriptures are explicit with respect to Israel, implicitly there is teaching contained within them which relates to the Church just as is the case throughout the whole of the Old Testament. The absence of explicit references to the Church in the Old Testament scriptures does not imply that the church is absent from the End Times. It simply means that revelation had not come to the prophets concerning the Church and therefore they make no clear reference to it. Thus, we need to read the Prophetic scriptures with a consciousness of the explicit New Testament teaching concerning the Church, particularly as those scriptures reveal the participation of the Church in the period known as the End Times.

It is also worth noting that time and space will not allow us to deal extensively with the Old Testament prophetic passages concerning the End Times. Thus, within this study we will pick out and summarise key themes which are contained within these scriptures.

Themes

Within the prophetic books of the Old Testament, seven key themes emerge and are addressed in different ways by the prophets at different times. These themes are as follows:

- The judgement of the nations.
- The judgement and restoration of Israel.
- The restoration of Jerusalem.
- The advent of the Messiah (First and Second).
- The rule of the Messiah from Jerusalem.
- The destruction of the earth.
- The new heavens and the new earth.

We will carry out our study of the Old Testament prophetic books following these themes.

The Judgement of the Nations

Within the prophetic books, the theme of judging the nations recurs many times. It is used both of specific nations and in a general sense of all nations.

A number of difficulties arise when interpreting these scriptures, the main one being prophetic foreshortening - the fact that prophecies concerning events contemporary with the prophet (or soon after the time in which he prophesied) occur in the same passages as events which are later or End Time events. The prophets were speaking into the situation that confronted them and many of the judgements cited by them were fulfilled, as detailed below, however, they also saw events which will be part of the End Time judgement of God upon all the nations of the earth.

This end time judgement is summarised in Isaiah 2:12-18 where it is made clear that 'a day of reckoning' is coming 'against everyone who is proud and lofty' (v.12) and that in that day 'the Lord alone will be exalted' (v.17). Thus, as we read these passages we must pick out the immediate from that which is reserved for the End Times.

We will deal first of all with specific national judgements that are spoken of by the prophets throughout the prophetic scriptures and then turn to the general judgement of all nations.

Ammon

Jeremiah 49:1-6 deals with judgement on Ammon, and specifically on the God Milcom or Molech. Ammon was first dealt a blow by Nebuchadnezzar in 582 BC in reprisal for the murder of Gedaliah (see Jeremiah 41) and later was invaded by tribes from the Arabian Desert who drove out the people of Moab, Ammon and Edom. Ezekiel refers to this event in Ezekiel 25:4-5 when he refers to 'the people of the east'. By the end of the century all three peoples (Moab, Ammon and Edom) had been driven out and their territory taken over. Ezekiel suggests that the reason for the judgement on Ammon is because they rejoiced over the fall of Jerusalem and specifically over the destruction of the temple (Ezekiel 25:3). Amos (Amos 1:13-15) suggests that the destruction is because of their violence towards Israel in order to increase their own territory. Zephaniah (Zephaniah 2: 8-11) assigns their destruction as arising from the fact that they have 'taunted and become arrogant against the people of the Lord of Hosts'.

Thus the judgement of Ammon is largely an historical event, however, verse 6 of Jeremiah 49 ends with a promise of restoration for Ammon similar to that give to Moab (see below).

Moab

In Isaiah chapters 15 and 16, Isaiah prophesies concerning the destruction of Moab which took place historically at the time of Saragon, the Assyrian king in 715BC. Within these verses we see a prophetic foreshadowing of the reign of the Messiah (16:5) as survivors from Moab appeal to the king of Judah for sanctuary (16:1-5).

Jeremiah 48 deals with a later destruction of Moab in some detail. This destruction occurred historically after the invasion and destruction of Philistia by Pharaoh Neco between 609 and 605BC and subsequently by Babylon after Carchemish. Finally, Moab, like Ammon, was overrun by 'the people of the east' (see above and also Ezekiel 25:10). Isaiah (Isaiah 15 & 16) refers to the destruction of Moab and gives the reason as their 'excessive pride' (16:6). Amos also prophesies concerning the destruction of Moab (Amos 2: 1-3). Zephaniah wraps up the judgement of Moab with that of Ammon (Zephaniah 2: 8-11) and again refers to the pride of Moab (and Ammon).

Again, chapter 48 of Jeremiah concludes with a promise of restoration for Moab 'in the latter days'.

Edom

Jeremiah 49:7-22 deals with judgement on Edom. As indicated above, this occurred within the 5th century as Edom was overrun by tribes from the Arabian Desert, and later by the Nabateans. However, in verse 14 we are given an indicator once more that Edom is the battleground where the nations will be gathered during the End Times. This is made clearer in Isaiah 34 where the destruction of Edom is associated with 'the Lord's indignation against all the nations' (see The Nations below).

The book of Obadiah parallels the judgements expressed in Jeremiah, however, Obadiah in verse 18 goes further, saying '...there will be no survivor of the house of Esau'. He gives the reason for Edom's complete destruction as their gloating over the destruction of Judah (v.12) and for 'violence to your brother Judah' (v.10). Amos mirrors Obadiah in Amos 1:11-12 in saying that the judgement is due to Edom's 'anger' against his brother. Ezekiel (Ezekiel 25:12-14) allocates the reason for the judgement of Edom as being due to the fact that they took revenge on Israel and saw Israel's demise as an opportunity (Ezekiel 35).

There is no promise here of an end time restoration for Edom, the reprobate brother of Israel.

Egypt

Isaiah chapters 19 and 20 deal with the judgement against Egypt. There is no specific destruction of Egypt prefigured here. From this point in history onwards a number of tyrants came against Egypt including Esarhaddon in 671 BC, Ashurbanipal in 667BC, Nebuchadnezzar in 586 BC, Cambyses in 525 BC, and Alexander the Great in 332 BC. Any one of these could be the 'cruel master' of verse 4. However, in verses 16 onwards of chapter 19 there is a shift with the use of the phrase 'in that day'. The remainder of this chapter deals with the end time salvation of Egypt and its position during the Millennium (see below).

The prophecy of Isaiah 20 is given an historical context as being when Philistia was destroyed by Saragon in 711 BC. It refers to the fact that Philistia depended on Egypt but was still defeated and its king given over by Egypt to Assyria.

Verses 1 to 26 of chapter 46 of Jeremiah deal with the historic defeat of Egypt which took place at the hands of Nebuchadnezzar, first at the battle of Carchemish in 605 BC, and finally with invasion in 568/7. The last phrase of verse 26, however, gives the promise of restoration for Egypt. This has previously been promised in Isaiah 19:19-25 where we see an End Time (millennial) alliance between Egypt, Assyria and Israel.

Ezekiel, in chapters 29 to 32 spends a great deal of time dealing with the fall of Egypt at the hands of Nebuchadnezzar and the Babylonians (29: 17-20, 30:20-26, 32: 11-15). In his day he was witnessing the end of a superpower which had been a significant player on the world scene for over a millennium. However, in Ezekiel 29:13-16, he hints at the restoration of Egypt to nation status, although without its previous power, 40 years after its destruction.

Philistia

Isaiah 14:29-32 (declared in 715BC) prophesies judgement on Philistia despite the recent death of Shalmeneser III in 721 BC (the 'broken rod' of verse 29) and the contemporary instability of Assyrian rule. Thus the instruction given to Philistia is not to rejoice because their destruction had thus been prophesied and historically came at the hand of Saragon, Shalmaneser's successor in 711 BC.

Jeremiah Chapter 47 foreshadows the invasion and destruction of Philistia by Pharaoh Neco between 609 and 605BC and subsequently by Babylon after Carchemish. Ezekiel 25:15-17 gives the reason for this judgement on Philistia as being because the Philistines 'have acted in revenge and have taken vengeance with scorn' upon Israel. Amos cites the reason for judgement on Philistia as being because they sold a population (although he does not state which) into slavery to Edom (1:6). Zephaniah (2:4-7) reiterates the absolute destruction of the Philistines, however, this refers to a time when this area of the Middle East will be 'for the remnant of the house of Judah'. At the time of writing, this land was still occupied by the Philistines (Palestinians) and therefore the prophecy foreshadows a time still to come.

In verses 5 to 7 of chapter 9 of Zechariah, judgement upon Philistia is reiterated; however, this prophecy was given some 80 years after Carchemish and therefore refers to a future devastation of this area. This foreshadows the invasion of Alexander the Great, particularly the reference to the destruction of Tyre in verse 5.

Tyre and Sidon

Isaiah 23 deals with the fall of Tyre and its devastating effect across the Mediterranean in places as far away as Tarshish (v. 6, i.e. Spain), Cyprus (v.12) and Egypt (v.5). The closing section of chapter 23 deals with the symbolic meaning of Tyre as the economic trade and prosperity centre of the world which ultimately will be used in the hand of God to bring wealth to 'those who dwell in the presence of the Lord' (v.18).

In addition to the other nations, Ezekiel contains a lengthy judgement on Tyre and Sidon. He begins with Tyre and with a denunciation of the city of Tyre for its opportunistic attitude towards the destruction of Jerusalem ('I shall be filled now that she is laid waste', 26:2). Clearly, Tyre saw Jerusalem's destruction as an opportunity for its own economic advantage. Amos states that Tyre 'delivered up an entire population to Edom' presumably for financial gain, and was therefore judged.

Ezekiel prophesied that 'many nations' (v.3) would come up against Tyre and that the outcome would be the complete destruction of Tyre. The first of these, he prophesied, would be Babylon under the command of Nebuchadnezzar. This indeed happened in a siege which lasted for 13 years and which, whilst not bringing about the destruction of Tyre, did result in the submission of Tyre to Babylonian rule. The final destruction of Tyre came at the hand of Alexander the Great, who built a causeway linking the offshore island of Tyre to the mainland, thus providing a means of access for his soldiers to overrun the city, resulting in the slaughter of the inhabitants. Zechariah also refers to this in Zechariah 9:2 to 4.

In chapters 27 and 28 of Ezekiel there follows a series of laments, firstly over the city of Tyre itself and secondly, over the King of Tyre. At the end of chapter 28, Ezekiel turns his attention to Sidon and refers to it as 'a prickling brier or a painful thorn' of which there will be no more for the house of Israel. This verse looks forward to the End Time position when all of Israel's enemies will be subjected to the returning king.

Ezekiel continues in verses 25 to 26 of chapter 28 to reinforce the fact that Israel will be re-gathered to the land and will live securely and in peace following God's judgement on the nations.

Damascus

In Isaiah 17, the prophet forewarns of the destruction of Damascus (allied with Ephraim (v.3)) that took place in 732 BC when Damascus fell after a ruinous siege. It was at this point that sovereignty departed from Damascus (v.3) as it was absorbed into the Assyrian empire.

Verses 23 to 27 of Jeremiah chapter 49 deal with judgement on Damascus (cf. Amos 1:3-5). This followed the battle of Carchemish when the whole region was overrun by Babylon. Amos picks up the theme of judgement against Damascus in Amos 1:3-5. He cites the reason for this judgement as being 'because they threshed Gilead with implements of sharp iron'. In other words, for coming against part of the territory on the east side of the Jordan that had been under Israel's control.

Kedar and Hazor

Isaiah 21:11-6 contains a prophecy concerning the Arabian tribes and their decimation at the hands of Senacherib for allying with Babylon. Specifically mentioned are Dumah, Arabia and Kedar.

Verses 28 to 33 of Jeremiah chapter 49 deal with the judgement upon Kedar and Hazor. Kedar was an Ishmaelite tribe (see Genesis 25:13 & 16) and Bright suggests that Hazor (hasor) was not the walled city in northern Palestine but rather a collective name for the 'haserim' or unwalled villages (v.31) of the Ishmaelite tribes. Clearly, in the passage (v.28) whichever places are being referred to, they were defeated by Nebuchadnezzar and thus the prophesied judgement came upon them.

Elam

Jeremiah 49:34-39 deals with the judgement upon Elam. Elam was situated at the head of the Persian Gulf. Ezra 4:9-10 refers to the fact that Susa (the winter capital of the Persian kings) was in Elam and that Elamites had been settled by Ashurbannipal, the Assyrian king, in Samaria. The Elamites were scattered, however, in Acts 2:9-11 it is mentioned that people from Elam were also witnesses to the Pentecostal outpouring suggesting that, despite being scattered, they had not lost their identity. This passage in Jeremiah concludes once again with a promise of restoration for Elam.

Assyria

Isaiah refers to the destruction of Assyria in chapter 14:24-27. Assyria of course had been responsible for the deportation of the northern tribes of Israel. By the time of the later prophets such as Jeremiah, this prophesied destruction had already been fulfilled by the hand of Nebuchadnezzar.

Nahum prophesies extensively concerning the destruction of Assyria and specifically of its capital, Nineveh, in chapters 2 and 3.

Ethiopia

Isaiah 18 deals with judgement on Ethiopia. At the time of the late 8th Century BC, during Hezekiah's reign, Ethiopia merged with Egypt under the 25th Dynasty, who were Ethiopians. Thus, what is prefigured here is the alliance of Palestinian states with Egypt which rebelled against Assyrian domination in 705 to 701 BC and which failed in their rebellion (c.f. also Zephaniah 2: 12).

Babylon

Isaiah refers to the destruction of Babylon in chapter 13 and 14. Verses 1 to 16 of chapter 13 deal with God's end time judgement of the nations (see below), however, verses 17 to 22 deal with the judgement against Babylon which commenced in BC 536 with the defeat of Babylon by Cyrus (the Medes are cited as the nation who were to bring judgement in this passage). Verses 19 to 22 describe the present day state of the ancient city of Babylon. The theme of Babylon's destruction is continued through chapter 14.

The destruction of Babylon is again prefigured in chapter 21 of Isaiah and again, the Medes and the Persians are cited as the destroyers (v.2). In verse 9, the phrase 'fallen, fallen is Babylon' occurs, which is picked up in Revelation 18:2 concerning the End Time destruction of Babylon the Great.

Isaiah returns to this theme in chapter 43:14-15 where he prophesies concerning the destruction of Babylon and again in chapter 46 where it is shown that Babylon's gods will bow down to the Lord (v.1-2) and in chapter 47 where again Babylon's doom in the midst of complacency is cited (v.8-9). The reason given for this doom is that Babylon did not show mercy towards Israel when they were given by the Lord into Babylon's hands (v.6). Instead, Babylon simply became proud and arrogant (v.7, 8, &10).

Chapters 50 and 51 of Jeremiah deal with the judgement upon Babylon, the state which had been used to fulfil God's prophesied judgement on so many other nations. In God's hand, Babylon had been his 'war-club' (51:20) with which he had shattered the nations. But God's judgement on Babylon is 'because of the evil that they have done in Zion before your eyes' (51:24).

Verse 9 of chapter 50 says, '...I am going to arouse and bring up against Babylon a horde of great nations from the land of the north.' The chapter goes on to speak of the destruction of Babylon (v.15, v.22-23, 26, et al). However, the historic fall of Babylon did not occur in this way. Instead, Cyrus walked into Babylon and took it peacefully. It was still very much intact in the days of Alexander the Great who died there. The destruction of Babylon into a 'heap of ruins' and 'a haunt of jackals'

(51:37) took place over many years and was due largely to the building of a new capital at Seleucia on the Tigris in 275 BC. This leads us to conclude that the destruction of Babylon referred to in these chapters has not yet occurred. Consideration of the passages concerning Babylon in Revelation 17 and 18 lead us to suggest that the destruction referred to here is an End Times event where Babylon is 'the embodiment of this world's corrupt power and glory and the archetypal opposite of Zion, the city of God.'[31] This is also suggested by verse 4-5 of chapter 50 which declares,

"In those days and at that time," declares the Lord, "the sons of Israel will come, both they and the sons of Judah as well; they will go along weeping as they go, and it will be the Lord their God they will seek. They will ask the way to Zion, turning their faces in its direction; they will come that they may join themselves to the Lord in an everlasting covenant that will not be forgotten."

Thus, the destruction of Babylon is placed at the same time as the final restoration of Israel back to God (c.f. 31:33-34, 50:20-21).

For consideration of the significance of Babylon see Chapter 12.

Magog, Rosh, Meshech and Tubal

Ezekiel chapters 38-39 deal with Magog, Rosh, Meshech and Tubal. For a discussion concerning these nations and their End Time significance, see Appendix 3. Suffice to say, they do not figure in the narrative by name until after the Millennium (see Revelation 20:8).

The Nations

Throughout the prophetic books of the Old Testament, frequent reference is made to God's judgement on the nations of the earth. We have dealt with those passages which refer to judgement on specific nations above, however, beyond this, it is clear that a general judgement upon all nations is foreseen.

In Isaiah 2:4 we are told that 'He will judge between the nations' and that after he has rendered judgement, they will no longer go to war. Isaiah 2:12 gives us the backdrop for this in stating, 'for the Lord of Hosts will have a day of reckoning against everyone who is proud and

[31] *Kidner p.149.*

lofty and against everyone who is lifted up that he may be abased'. This is restated in Isaiah 13:11. Verses 1 to 16 of Isaiah chapter 13 give an overview of the 'day of the Lord' and the destruction on a global scale associated with it.

Zechariah 1:15 gives the reason for this judgement as follows: 'I am very angry with the nations who are at ease for while I was only a little angry (against Jerusalem) they furthered the disaster'.

This theme is also alluded to in Isaiah 34:8 which states, 'For the Lord has a day of vengeance, a year of recompense for the cause of Zion'. Isaiah 17:12-14 indicates that this judgement includes the destruction of the nations who 'plunder' and 'pillage' Judah.

Joel 3: 3 gives the reason for the judgement as being against those who 'have scattered (my people) among the nations and they have divided up My land. They have cast lots for my people'. In other words the judgement is given for the manner in which the nations of the world have treated the people and land of Israel. Obadiah 15 declares that this judgement will be retributive ('as you have done it will be done to you').

Isaiah 24 paints a picture of devastation of the earth 'in that day'[32] (v.21). Included within this passage is the notion that the earth itself will be physically devastated ('Behold the Lord lays the earth waste, devastates it, distorts it and scatters its inhabitants' (v.1)), and the people on the earth will also be destroyed ('Therefore the inhabitants of the earth are burned, and few men are left' (v.6). See also Isaiah 13:12). In Zephaniah 3:8, the prophet also portrays the earth being devastated ('for all the earth will be devoured by the fire of My zeal').

Isaiah chapters 33 and 34 pick up the theme of the judgement of 'all the nations' (34:2) and identifies the location of this judgement as Edom (34:5-6). This is confirmed in Isaiah 63:1 where we see the Messiah coming to Jerusalem from Edom with the blood of the nations sprinkled on his robes on 'the day of vengeance'. In Joel 3:2 and 12, the location of this judgement of the nations is identified as 'the valley of Jehoshaphat. The name 'Jehoshaphat' means 'God judges' and thus Joel is not referring necessarily to a geographical valley but a figurative valley

[32] *'in that day' or 'the day of the Lord' are terms used frequently throughout the Old Testament to indicate the day when the Messiah will come to reign in Jerusalem and deal with the nations of the earth.*

where the judgement of God against the nations will take place[33] (see also verse 14 where the locations is referred to as 'the valley of decision').

What is clear from the above passages is that the nations will be gathered into one place for judgement (see also Zephaniah 3:8), and the judgement will be specifically against the armies of the nations (Joel 3:9-10) but that the outcome of this judgement will be catastrophic across the earth (see also Isaiah 24:1-6).

In Joel 3:13 we also see the imagery of the wine press and the harvest being gathered for judgement using a sickle (c.f. Revelation 14:14-20). This again ties in with the image of the Messiah coming from Edom with blood-spattered garments having 'trodden the winepress alone' (Isaiah 63: 1-4).

In Isaiah 13:10 we have the familiar image of the sun being darkened and the moon not giving its light (v.10 cf. Matthew 24:29) and the reason given for this is that God 'will punish the world for its evil and the wicked for their iniquity.' This image occurs repeatedly in the Old and New Testaments (see also Isaiah 24:3, Ezekiel 32:7, Joel 2:10, 2:31, 3:15, Matthew 24:29, Mark 13:24, Luke 21:25, Acts 2:20, Revelation 6:12, 8:12).

In Jeremiah 30:10-11, we have the following words:

> *'Fear not, O Jacob My servant,' declares the LORD, 'and do not be dismayed, O Israel; For behold, I will save you from afar And your offspring from the land of their captivity. And Jacob will return and will be quiet and at ease, and no one will make him afraid. 'For I am with you,' declares the LORD, 'to save you; for I will destroy completely all* the nations where I *have scattered you, only I will not destroy you completely. But I will chasten you justly and will by no means leave you unpunished.'*

[33] *'Jehoshaphat, Valley of, the name given to the valley situated between Jerusalem and the Mount of Olives, which in modern times has been used by the Jews as a burying-ground. There is a typical use of the word, in a sense of divine judgements upon the enemies of God and his people (Joel 3:2, 12). In this valley Jehoshaphat overthrew the united enemies of Israel (2 Chronicles 20:26, A.V. "Valley of Berechah").*
From the Fourth century A.D. the Valley of Jehoshaphat has been identified with the Kidron. This identification is based on Joel 3:2, 12 and particularly Zecheriah 13, but since no actual valley bore this name in pre-Christian antiquity, Joel's prophetic employment of it is figurative of the place where the judgement of the nations will take place prior to Christ's Second Advent and the setting up of the millennial Kingdom.' Unger p.564

This sums up the judgement upon the nations and also indicates our next two themes: judgement upon Israel and the restoration and salvation of Israel.

The Judgement of Israel

The Old Testament prophetic books are full of passages containing both the judgement and restoration of Israel. In most cases the proclamation of coming judgement was the reason for the prophet being raised up. Rather than going through all of the prophecies in detail here, the point of greater pertinence is the reason for the judgement on Israel. This is summed up in the parable of Isaiah 5:1-7. In this parable, the prophet likens Israel to the vineyard of the Lord. The reason for the judgement is given in verse 2: 'Then he expected it to produce good grapes but it produced only worthless ones' and confirmed in verse 7: 'He looked for justice, but behold, bloodshed; for righteousness, but behold, a cry of distress'.

The consequences of this are given in the remainder of the parable. Essentially, the Lord will 'lay it waste' (i.e. the land of Israel) and this occurred in the subsequent exile (c.f. v.13), of Israel and Judah at the hands of the Assyrians and Babylonians respectively.

In Matthew 21:33-44, Jesus draws upon this parable whilst talking to the Chief Priests. In his version, he likens the custodians of Judaism (priests, scribes and Pharisees) to the vine-growers who ultimately reject him. As the Kingdom of God transfers into the hands of the Church (those bringing forth the fruits of repentance[34]), God deals with a remnant of Israel who accept the Messiah and his salvation by faith. The rest of the nation is under judgement and hence, the land has lain fallow for nearly 2000 years. However, with the restoration of the Jews to the land and the re-establishing of the nation of Israel in 1947, we see God's preparation for his End Time restoration of the Jewish people to faith (see below and also Romans 11 and Chapter 1 of this book).

It is worth reiterating that the judgement upon Israel has been at God's hand, but in the last 2000 years, the nations have added to that judgement through relentless persecution, culminating in the Final Solution of the Nazis. Zechariah 1:15 confirms that the reason God will

[34] *The Church, if it does not 'bring forth the fruits of repentance' puts itself under judgement in the same way as the leaders of Israel did. See also Romans 11:17-24 for Paul's discussion of this.*

pour out his wrath upon the nations at the return of Christ is because of their adding to his judgement.

The Restoration of Israel

Despite the fact that God judged Israel because 'they have rejected the Law of the Lord of Hosts and despised the word of the Holy One of Israel' (Isaiah 5:24), there is the promise of Israel's restoration on the return of the Messiah:

Isaiah 11:11-12 says,

> *In that day the Lord will reach out his hand a second time to reclaim the remnant that is left of his people from Assyria, from Lower Egypt, from Upper Egypt, from Cush, from Elam, from Babylonia, from Hamath and from the islands of the sea. He will raise a banner for the nations and gather the exiles of Israel; he will assemble the scattered people of Judah from the four quarters of the earth.*

This is confirmed in Isaiah 35: 10 '...and the ransomed of the LORD will return. They will enter Zion with singing; everlasting joy will crown their heads. Gladness and joy will overtake them, and sorrow and sighing will flee away'; also in Isaiah 12:1 'In that day you will say: "I will praise you, O LORD. Although you were angry with me, your anger has turned away and you have comforted me"'.

Again, Isaiah 14: 1-2 says:

> *The LORD will have compassion on Jacob; once again he will choose Israel and will settle them in their own land. Aliens*[35] *will join them and unite with the house of Jacob. Nations will take them and bring them to their own place. And the house of Israel will possess the nations as menservants and maidservants in the LORD's land. They will make captives of their captors and rule over their oppressors.*

Clearly a gathering of Israel back to the land is envisaged:

> *In that day the LORD will thresh from the flowing Euphrates to the Wadi of Egypt, and you, O Israelites, will be gathered up one by one. And in that day a great trumpet will sound. Those who were perishing in Assyria and those who were exiled in Egypt will come and worship the LORD on the holy mountain in Jerusalem. (Isaiah 27:12-13) See also Isaiah 43:1-7.*

[35] *Perhaps an oblique reference to Christ uniting all his people as one flock during His messianic reign (c.f. Ephesians 2:19).*

Following the restoration of Israel, we see in Isaiah 30:23-26 a restored land as well:

> *He will also send you rain for the seed you sow in the ground, and the food that comes from the land will be rich and plentiful. In that day your cattle will graze in broad meadows. The oxen and donkeys that work the soil will eat fodder and mash, spread out with fork and shovel. In the day of great slaughter, when the towers fall, streams of water will flow on every high mountain and every lofty hill. The moon will shine like the sun, and the sunlight will be seven times brighter, like the light of seven full days, when the LORD binds up the bruises of his people and heals the wounds he inflicted'.*

It is clear from this passage that the restoration of the land occurs during the time following 'great slaughter', i.e. the judgement of the nations.

Isaiah 43:17 tells us that God's salvation of Israel will be everlasting: 'But Israel will be saved by the LORD with an everlasting salvation; you will never be put to shame or disgraced, to ages everlasting'.

In Jeremiah chapter 3:14-17 we see the restoration predicted once more:

> *...And I will bring you to Zion. Then I will give you shepherds after My own heart, who will feed you on knowledge and understanding. ...At that time they will call Jerusalem 'The Throne of the LORD,' and all the nations will be gathered to it, to Jerusalem, for the name of the LORD; nor will they walk anymore after the stubbornness of their evil heart. In those days the house of Judah will walk with the house of Israel, and they will come together from the land of the north to the land that I gave your fathers as an inheritance.*

In Jeremiah 16:14-21 and 23:7-8, once more we have prophesied the re-gathering of Israel to the land. Whilst this was true of the post-exilic period, it seems that a wide scattering is envisaged in these verses ('from the north land and from all the countries where I had driven them').

In Jeremiah 31:1-40, we see the restoration detailed once more; however, it is of particular significance that the basis of this restoration is the new covenant (31:31). It is clear from this passage that 'they will all know me', i.e. the Lord, which is confirmed by Paul in Romans 11:25. Ezekiel picks up this theme once more in Ezekiel 11:14-21 and 16:60-63 where the restoration is associated with a change of heart for Israel (see also

Ezekiel 36:22-38, Hosea 2:29, 14:4, Joel 2:19, 3:18, Amos 9:11-15, Micah 2:12-13, Zephaniah 3: 12-13).

Once more, in Jeremiah 46:27-28, we see the restoration of Israel promised coincidental with the judgement of the nations. This is confirmed again in Ezekiel 28:25-26.

Ezekiel 39:25-29 recounts not only Israel's physical restoration to the land but also the restoring of their fortunes. This is coincident with God pouring out his Spirit upon them (v.29)

In Zephaniah 3:14-17 we see the restoration as being associated with an end of the punishment of Israel:

> *"Sing, O Daughter of Zion; shout aloud, O Israel! Be glad and rejoice with all your heart, O Daughter of Jerusalem! The LORD has taken away your punishment, he has turned back your enemy. The LORD, the King of Israel, is with you; never again will you fear any harm. On that day they will say to Jerusalem, "Do not fear, O Zion; do not let your hands hang limp. The LORD your God is with you, he is mighty to save. He will take great delight in you, he will quiet you with his love, he will rejoice over you with singing. "The sorrows for the appointed feasts I will remove from you; they are a burden and a reproach to you. At that time I will deal with all who oppressed you; I will rescue the lame and gather those who have been scattered. I will give them praise and honour in every land where they were put to shame. At that time I will gather you; at that time I will bring you home. I will give you honour and praise among all the peoples of the earth when I restore your fortunes before your very eyes," says the LORD.*

The Restoration of Jerusalem

Implicit within the restoration of Israel is the restoration of Jerusalem (Zion). Isaiah makes it very clear that God's purpose will be to restore Jerusalem and, make it the place of Jesus' throne.

Isaiah 40:2 say,

> *Speak tenderly to Jerusalem, and proclaim to her that her hard service has been completed, that her sin has been paid for, that she has received from the LORD's hand double for all her sins.*

This theme of the restoration of Jerusalem is repeated frequently in

Isaiah (51:3, 11, 52:1-10, 60:1-22, 62:1-12, Isaiah 66:10-17)

This restoration is summarised in verses 11 & 12 of Isaiah 62:

> *The LORD has made proclamation to the ends of the earth: "Say to the Daughter of Zion, 'See, your Saviour comes! See, his reward is with him, and his recompense accompanies him'. They will be called the Holy People, the Redeemed of the LORD; and you will be called Sought After, the City No Longer Deserted.*

In Micah 4:1-2, we see Jerusalem established not only as the political seat of rule for the Messiah (see below), but also as the religious centre of the earth where people will come from all nations to worship the Lord:

> *In the last days the mountain of the LORD's temple will be established as chief among the mountains; it will be raised above the hills, and peoples will stream to it. Many nations will come and say, "Come, let us go up to the mountain of the LORD, to the house of the God of Jacob. He will teach us his ways, so that we may walk in his paths." The law will go out from Zion, the word of the LORD from Jerusalem.*

The Advent of the Messiah (First and Second)

Isaiah is full of references to the Messiah. However, once more we encounter the issue of prophetic foreshortening where the first and second comings of the Messiah are often found in the same passage, for example, Isaiah 9:6-7. However, wherever the second coming is envisaged, the description is one of judgement for the nations or redemption for Israel (see Isaiah 59:20 and 63:1-6).

Isaiah 42:1-4 gives us a clear insight into the purpose of Jesus return: to bring 'justice to the nations' and 'justice on earth'. There are two aspects to this: firstly, that he will judge the nations for their injustice to Israel (see above), and secondly, that he will bring about His just rule upon the earth.

It is clear from Jeremiah 23:5-6 that the Messiah's coming is associated with a time of peace for Israel and a righteous reign, not just for Israel, but for the whole earth. See also Jeremiah 33:15, Micah 5:2-5 and Hosea 3:4-5.

In Ezekiel 20:33 we have the promise of God not only to bring back the nation of Israel from all the places where they have been scattered but also to 'be king over' them (see also Ezekiel 34:23-24 and Ezekiel 37:24-28).

Malachi 3:1-5 tells us that the Messiah will not only come to Jerusalem but also to the temple. This passage carries with it the notion of judgement for all the unrighteous of Israel as well.

The Rule of the Messiah from Jerusalem

As mentioned above, the advent of the Messiah is associated with a period during which He will reign in righteousness upon the earth. The extent and timing of this period is dependent on the view taken by the individual regarding the Millennium (see Chapter 3). Also, many have debated whether this is a literal reign from Jerusalem over Israel and from there over the world, or whether we should take the references to 'Israel' and 'Zion' as typical references to the reign of the Messiah over His New Covenant people made up of Jews and Gentiles who have accepted his salvation on the basis of faith. Once more, the view taken on this is dependent on the position one assumes with regard to God's purposes for Israel (see Chapter 1).

The following assumes that we take the prophecies literally concerning Israel and the nations (as we have above with regard to the judgement of the nations, and the judgement and restoration of Israel).

Isaiah makes much reference to the reign of the Messiah on earth. It is clear from a number of passages that the seat of that reign will be Jerusalem and that following the outpouring of his wrath upon the nations, nations will come up to Jerusalem yearly to pay homage. This is indicated in Isaiah 2:1-4 as follows:

- The mountain of the House of the Lord (Mount Zion) will be the 'chief of mountains' (see also Micah 4:1-2).
- People will come to it from all over the world to learn about the ways of God
- God's word will go forth from Jerusalem

Zechariah 14:16 gives confirmation of the coming of the nations annually up to Jerusalem (see previous chapter). In this scripture it indicates also a celebration of the Feast of Booths.

Isaiah 9 verse 7 tells us, concerning the Messiah,

> *Of the increase of his government and peace there will be no end. He will reign on David's throne and over his Kingdom, establishing and upholding it with justice and righteousness from that time on and forever.*

There are two keys here: firstly, that Jesus will reign on David's throne. This positions the seat of His throne as Jerusalem. Secondly, that His reign will be everlasting and will be typified by justice and righteousness. These notions are also confirmed in the following passages: Isaiah 11:1-5, 16:5, 32:1-20, 33: 20-22, 24:23.

Some of the scriptures in Isaiah and Jeremiah ostensibly concern the post-exilic return of Israel to the land (534 BC following), however, these scriptures hint that the historic restoration of Israel is not meant exclusively since they contain elements which are still to be fulfilled. Jeremiah 32 is one such scripture where the post-exilic people are described as a people who remain faithful to God 'always', however, we know that in their subsequent rejection of the Messiah, they have once more acquired the need for restoration.

In Ezekiel 34:25-31 we see the effects of the righteous reign of the Messiah upon Israel - removal of dangerous beasts from the land, blessing on the crops, security without fear, and they will no longer be 'a prey to the nations' (v.28), These themes are re-emphasised in Ezekiel 36.

Amos 9:13-15 refers once more to the blessing which will be on the land during the period of the Messiah's reign:

> *"The days are coming," declares the LORD, "when the reaper will be overtaken by the ploughman and the planter by the one treading grapes. New wine will drip from the mountains and flow from all the hills. I will bring back my exiled people Israel; they will rebuild the ruined cities and live in them. They will plant vineyards and drink their wine; they will make gardens and eat their fruit. I will plant Israel in their own land, never again to be uprooted from the land I have given them," says the LORD your God.*

Obadiah 21 recounts quite simply that at that time, 'the Kingdom will be the LORD's' (v.21).

Micah 4:1-8 tells us that this will be a time of peace on the earth when the people will 'beat their swords into plowshares and their spears into pruning hooks' (see also Isaiah 2:4 and compare with Joel 3:10 where the opposite is the case as the nations come up against the Lord for judgement). Micah goes on to say, 'Nation will not take up sword against nation, nor will they train for war anymore' (v.4).

In verse 6 of chapter 4, Micah says 'The LORD will rule over them in Mount Zion from that day and forever', thus positioning the seat of the Messiah's rule eternally.

The Destruction of the Earth

A theme which, again, is repeated in Isaiah is that of the destruction of the earth. This is summed up in Isaiah 24:1-3, although the whole of Isaiah 24 is on this theme:

> *See, the LORD is going to lay waste the earth and devastate it; he will ruin its face and scatter its inhabitants- it will be the same for priest as for people, for master as for servant, for mistress as for maid, for seller as for buyer, for borrower as for lender, for debtor as for creditor. The earth will be completely laid waste and totally plundered. The LORD has spoken this word.*

Zephaniah also makes reference to this in Chapter 1:2-3:

> *"I will sweep away everything from the face of the earth," declares the LORD. "I will sweep away both men and animals; I will sweep away the birds of the air and the fish of the sea. The wicked will have only heaps of rubble when I cut off man from the face of the earth," declares the LORD*

However, the hope is in the final act of the Lord, which is the creation of a new heavens and earth.

The New Heavens and the New Earth.

Isaiah 65:17 states clearly that God will create a 'new heavens and a new earth'. The following scriptures summarise this theme:

> *Isaiah 11:6-9: The wolf will live with the lamb, the leopard will lie down with the goat, the calf and the lion and the yearling together; and a little child will lead them. The cow will feed with the bear, their young will lie down together, and the lion will eat straw like the ox. The infant will play near the hole of the cobra, and the young child put his hand into the*

viper's nest. They will neither harm nor destroy on all my holy mountain, for the earth will be full of the knowledge of the LORD as the waters cover the sea.

Isaiah 25: 6-8: On this mountain the LORD Almighty will prepare a feast of rich food for all peoples, a banquet of aged wine- the best of meats and the finest of wines. On this mountain he will destroy the shroud that enfolds all peoples, the sheet that covers all nations; he will swallow up death forever. The Sovereign LORD will wipe away the tears from all faces; he will remove the disgrace of his people from all the earth. The LORD has spoken.

Isaiah 65: 17-24: "Behold, I will create new heavens and a new earth. The former things will not be remembered, nor will they come to mind. But be glad and rejoice forever in what I will create, for I will create Jerusalem to be a delight and its people a joy. I will rejoice over Jerusalem and take delight in my people; the sound of weeping and of crying will be heard in it no more.

"Never again will there be in it an infant who lives but a few days, or an old man who does not live out his years; he who dies at a hundred will be thought a mere youth; he who fails to reach a hundred will be considered accursed. They will build houses and dwell in them; they will plant vineyards and eat their fruit. No longer will they build houses and others live in them, or plant and others eat. For as the days of a tree, so will be the days of my people; my chosen ones will long enjoy the works of their hands. They will not toil in vain or bear children doomed to misfortune; for they will be a people blessed by the LORD, they and their descendants with them. Before they call I will answer; while they are still speaking I will hear. The wolf and the lamb will feed together, and the lion will eat straw like the ox, but dust will be the serpent's food. They will neither harm nor destroy on all my holy mountain," says the LORD.

Finally, Isaiah 66:22 says that the new heavens and the new earth will 'endure before me', i.e. will be everlasting.

Summary

We have seen in this chapter how, in the extensive material of the Old

Testament prophets there are a number of recurring themes. All of them point to the fact that God still has a place in his purposes for physical Israel, which will be worked out at the close of the age. These purposes include Israel's restoration to the land, the judgement of the nations of the world, the coming of the Messiah, the spiritual restoration of Israel, the millennial reign of the Messiah and the new heavens and the new earth.

Clearly these things have not yet taken place. Any attempt to spiritualise these events takes us into dangerous territory and therefore the best approach is to take them as literal and physical events that will occur upon the earth and seek to fit them into the framework for the End Times given within the clear teaching of the New Testament. This we will attempt to do throughout the remainder of this book.

Chapter 10

Revelation I: Overview of the Book of Revelation

Introduction

Having considered the body of Old Testament prophetic and apocalyptic material found in Daniel and Zechariah, and the remaining prophetic material in the other Old Testament prophetic books, we now turn our attention to the New Testament apocalyptic material contained within the book of Revelation.

In the book of Revelation all previous prophecy concerning the End Times converges. The approach taken in this present study is, wherever possible, to consider the imagery portrayed within the book of Revelation by drawing upon previous occurrences of this imagery in other parts of scripture. As we have studied the Old Testament writings we have already indicated some of these occurrences and these will be considered below.

The book of Revelation can be approached in a number of different ways. Whichever way we approach it, it gives a splendid finish to the whole Bible and carries a wonderful symmetry with the book of Genesis. This is indicated in summary form in Table 1 below.

Table 1: Comparison of Genesis and Revelation

Genesis	Revelation
The Earth is created (1: 1)	The Earth passes away (21:1)
Sun and Moon appear (1:14-19)	Sun and Moon pass away (21:23)
There is a garden which is the home for Man (2:8)	There is a city which is the home for the nations (21:9-27)
There is the marriage of the First Adam (2:18-24)	There is the Marriage of the Last Adam (19:7-9)
The great enemy Satan appears (3:1)	The great enemy Satan is destroyed (19:20-20:10)
There is the inauguration of sorrow and suffering, the first sob and the first tear. (3:17-19)	There is no more suffering and no more pain, and all tears are wiped away (21:1-2)
The curse which comes because of sin is uttered (3:17-19)	There shall be no more curse (21:3)
We see Man driven away from the Tree of Life (3:24)	We see Man welcomed back with the Tree of Life at his disposal (21:2)

The word 'revelation' (Gk. Apokalypsis) literally means 'an uncovering or unveiling'[36]. Thus it is a book written to be understood because it is the revelation of Jesus Christ himself (Rev. 1:1), given to John. John goes on to say that anyone who reads it and understands it will be 'blessed' (1:3).

This book is the consummation of Biblical prophecy in which all that has gone before is revealed. Its chief themes are the events immediately preceding the second coming of Christ, the establishment of the Millennial Kingdom and finally, the eternal state following the judgements.

Drawing upon our studies in Daniel (especially Daniel 9:27, which deals with the Antichrist in the final 7 years of history), we can summarise

[36] *Unger p.922*

this End Time period as follows:

- There are two parts of 3 ½ years in duration during this final period.
- The start of the final 7 years is when the Antichrist makes a 'firm covenant' with Israel. The covenant will be broken half way through the time of tribulation and the sacrifices of Israel will be caused to cease (which pre-supposes that they have started by then and that the temple has been rebuilt – Rev 11:2).
- The Antichrist will set up a statue or image of some kind 'on the wing of abomination' (the pinnacle of the temple). The worship of the Antichrist will begin with the setting up of his image in some form in the temple.
- In verse 27 of Daniel 9 we are told that he makes desolation on the Jews (c.f. Matt 24:15-22), until the complete destruction decreed on the Antichrist is poured out.

Having drawn this summary from the book of Daniel to give us some essential anchor points for the period of the End Times, we will now review the book of Revelation.

Revelation 1-22

Components

In this book we have a number of components. The following is a definition of each of these without any attempt to put them in order:

- **The Great Tribulation:** *Last 7 years of history before Christ returns during which time all hell will break loose on earth, the Antichrist will arise, etc.*
- **The Unholy Trinity:** *Satan, The Antichrist and the False Prophet.*
- **The Two Witnesses:** *Messengers sent from God to oppose the Antichrist during the last 3 ½ years of the Tribulation.*
- **Babylon the Great:** *World Religious and Economic system.*
- **The Judgements:** *The Seals, The Trumpets and the Bowls which combined are God's wrath poured out on an unrepentant world.*
- **The Rapture:** *The catching up and transformation of the Church. The timing of this event is the subject of much debate as we saw in Chapter 3.*

- **The Coming of the King:** *The Return of Christ.*
- **Post Second Coming Events:** *The Millennium, the Judgements, the Doom of Satan, the Resurrections, the New Heaven and the New Earth.*

Outline of the Book

The following is an outline of the Book:

Revelation 1:

- John introduces the book which is: The Revelation of Jesus Christ to John.
- We see the great vision of Christ (1:12-20)

Revelation 2 to 3

- Letters to the seven Churches (Ephesus, Smyrna, Pergamum, Thyatira, Sardis, Philadelphia, Laodicea).
- Dispensationalists would say that these seven churches represent seven distinct ages of the Church through history from the Early Church through to the End Time Church just prior to the rapture[37]. Thus the Laodicean church is apostate (lukewarm). The downside of this view is that it says that we are now in the Laodicean age and that there is no hope for the Church – it will simply become more and more apostate until Christ returns to snatch away a few desperate Christians. Whilst it is clear from scripture that there will be a 'falling away' towards the end that does not permit us to adopt a negative and introverted attitude, but rather to do as Christ suggests in Revelation 3:19: 'be zealous and repent'. This is a time for zeal not withdrawal.
- An alternative view to the Dispensationalist position is that they are a message to the Church in all ages. John Stott[38] suggests that 'the seven churches of Asia, though historical, represent the local churches of all ages and of all lands'. In Revelation 1:11, Jesus tells John to send the revelation he is to receive to all the churches. Since the revelation deals with the End Times it is relevant for all churches everywhere who are awaiting the coming of the Lord. The 7 churches are representative of churches which can be seen at all times in all locations and the

[37] *See Unger, p.924 for a summary of these ages from a dispensational perspective.*
[38] *Stott p.8*

warning given to each one is therefore relevant to us all.

Revelation 4 to 11

- These chapters cover the full sweep of the End Times – the last 7 years.
- Rightfully it begins at the throne of God (chapter 4). The emphasis changes from earth to Heaven and we see what the throne of God is like.
- Chapter 5 reveals the book with seven seals and the fact that only the Lamb (Jesus himself) is worthy to open the seals. 'Worthy is the Lamb who was slain....to Him who sits on the throne and to the Lamb....' (v.12-13)
- Chapter 6 covers the opening of the first 6 seals. We see the Four Horsemen of the Apocalypse (Revelation). These seals speak of events which take place in the last 7 years and are the pouring out of the judgement of God upon the earth which will bring about its destruction, as prophesied (see Chapter 8 above).
- In Chapter 7 there is an interlude and we see a picture of those who survive the Tribulation – 144,000 from Israel and a multitude of believers from all other nations (v.14).
- In Chapter 8 - 9 we have the Seventh Seal which releases the Seven Trumpet judgements.
- In Chapter 10 we have the Angel and the Book and specific directions to John not to write down what the thunder says. Note should be taken of verse 7 of this chapter which reads 'but in the days of the voice of the Seventh Angel (the one who will blow the Seventh Trumpet)...then the mystery of God is finished, as He preached to His servants the prophets' What is the mystery (musterion: lit. 'open secret') of God? According to Ephesians 3:1-10 it is that salvation is available to both Jews and Gentiles through Jesus Christ, and that in bringing the two factions together into one body, the Church, God reveals his many-coloured wisdom to the 'rulers and authorities in heavenly places'. In other words, as the Seventh Trumpet is blown, the work of the gospel is completed and the mystery of God is fully revealed because the King himself is about to return (see 11:15).
- In verses 1 to 14 of chapter 11, we see the Two Witnesses who

testify during the latter half of the Tribulation (3 ½ years). This is out of character with the rest of the first half of Revelation and could sit in the second half, but God has put it here for a reason. We will look at the Witnesses in more detail in chapter 12.

- Finally in Revelation 11, The Seventh Trumpet sounds. This is at Christ's return and we are told of a number of things which will occur at this time:
  * The Kingdom of the world will become the Kingdom of our Lord and of His Christ.
  * He begins to reign.
  * His wrath is to be poured out against the 'enraged' nations.
  * The dead are to be judged.
  * The bondservants, the prophets and the saints are to be rewarded.
  * Those who destroy the earth will be destroyed.

All of these things are developed in more detail in the subsequent chapters of Revelation.

Revelation 12 to 16

- In chapters 12 to 16 the narrative laid out in chapters 4 to 11 is expanded and additional details are filled in for us of what has taken place with the opening of the Seals and the sounding of the Trumpets.
- The Woman in 12:1-2 represents Israel bringing forth Christ.
- The imagery of verse 3 of chapter 12 is of Satan taking a third of the Angelic hosts with him when he fell. This event took place prior to the creation of the universe but clearly identifies the dragon for us. In verse 4 we see him waiting to devour the child, just as he tried to destroy Christ through Herod the Great and through the crucifixion, but he (Christ) was 'caught up to God and to His throne' at the ascension.
- In verse 6 we jump from 2000 years ago to half way through the Tribulation. We know that in the persecution of Israel during the Tribulation, Israel will flee to Edom, Moab and Ammon (modern day Jordan) for 3 ½ years (1260 days) – see Daniel 11:41.
- In verse 7, we see that Satan is thrown down to earth for this last period of time, hence, 'knowing he only has a short time', this is a time during which great evil is unleashed upon the earth.

- Verses 13-14 repeat verse 6: the response of the Dragon to being cast out of heaven is to persecute the Jews and then to persecute all Christians who are alive on the earth at that time (v.17).
- In verse 15 to 16, we see Satan unleashing an army against Israel, but the earth intervenes - whether this is a physical earthquake which destroys the army or some other intervention we are not told. Suffice to say, Israel is rescued.
- Chapter 13 picks up on the rise of the last Empire and the actions of the Unholy Trinity. We have already considered much of this in chapter 7, and the remainder we will pick up in chapter 12.
- Chapter 14 alludes to the remnant of Israel saved from the Tribulation (v.1-5), the gospel to be preached (v.6) and the judgement to follow (v.7). Once again we are at the end of the Tribulation. We also see indicated the doom of Babylon (v.8), the doom of those who worship the beast (v.9-13), and the judgement of God on the nations (see 11:14 -18, c.f. Joel 3:13).
- In chapter 15 we see announced the final part of the wrath of God on the earth to be poured out in Six Bowls. These also take place during the Great Tribulation. In chapter 16 we see these poured out on the earth and add to its destruction.
- The battle of Armageddon is mentioned in 16:13-16, and finally, with the seventh bowl of wrath, the wrath of God is complete.

Chapters 17 to 18

These are concerned with the fall of Babylon. In the context of the whole book it appears a little unbalanced that the fall of Babylon is dedicated two chapters. We will consider Babylon in chapter 12.

Revelation 19

Chapter 19 begins to pull together the end of the Tribulation with the fourfold Hallelujah, the Marriage of the Lamb, and the coming of Christ. With this latter event we see the detail of His coming, and the doom of the Beast and the False Prophet.

Revelation 20 to 22

- In chapter 20 we see Satan, bound for 1,000 years, released and then doomed forever. This is the only place in scripture where the notion of a millennium is explicitly mentioned.
- We also see the first resurrection (20:5).
- We then see the Judgement (20:11-15).
- We are now back in sequence and we see the New Heaven and the New Earth created. We see the New Jerusalem coming down out of Heaven. This is not a literal city but the people of God (see Hebrews 12:22).
- In Chapter 22 we see the River and the tree of Life and we are left with a vision of a glorious future.
- Chapter 21 verses 10-21 include the final remarks of the Lord Jesus and he declares that 'these things are for the churches' and that 'I am coming quickly'.

Come Lord Jesus!

Chapter 11

Revelation II: Seals, Trumpets and Bowls - The Judgements of God upon the Earth

Introduction

In the book of Revelation, we see God's judgement poured out upon the earth. This is clearly the result of God withholding judgement for millennia, however, during the last days, he unleashes it in full fury. It is, perhaps, difficult to reconcile our view of God as a benign, loving father with the notion of God as judge, allowing such horror to come to the earth. Ultimately, we know that God is just and therefore, if he chooses to judge the world in this way, clearly it deserves to be judged.

The course of God's judgements upon the earth during the seven years of the Tribulation covers twelve chapters in the Book of Revelation. This is because, while the judgements are being poured out, certain other things are happening both in heaven and on the earth. For instance, chapter 7:1-17 is a parenthesis between the sixth and seventh seal. Chapters 10:1 to 11:14 are another parenthesis between the sixth and seventh trumpet. Chapters 12:1-14:20 are a discontinuity between the trumpets and bowls.

So then, the seals themselves cover Revelation 6:1-17 and 8:1-6. The trumpet judgements cover Revelation 8:7-9:21 and 11:15-19, and the bowl judgements cover Revelation 15:1-16:21.

During this time God will despatch: "Those destined for death, to death; And those destined for the sword, to the sword; And those destined for famine, to famine; And those destined for captivity, to captivity." (Jeremiah 15:2, c.f. Revelation 13:10).

Keys to help us understand these chapters:

In order to help us understand these various judgements, the following keys are given which provide a framework of interpretation.

1. The events in these chapters cover the seven years of the Tribulation, although some occur during the first three and one half years, some at the midway point, and others in the second three and one half years.
2. The Book of Revelation, like the rest of the Bible, must be taken literally where it is at all possible. When the language of a passage cannot possibly be literal, and it is clear from the passage itself, as well as from other corroborating scriptures that it is figurative, we must take it figuratively. It must be remembered, however, that all figurative language conveys literal truth. For instance, in Revelation 12:1-2, the woman is a symbol for Israel and she is travailing with labour pains. Whilst it is clear that a symbol cannot travail literally and therefore the imagery is figurative, Israel will travail (suffer) and did travail at the hands of Herod when the Messiah was born into the world.
3. There are two main purposes in God's agenda for the Tribulation:
    a. To make an end of wickedness and wicked ones. (Isaiah 13:9, Isaiah 24:19-20, and Daniel 9:24).
    b. To shatter 'the power of the holy people': to break the power or the stubborn will of the Jewish nation (Daniel 12:5-7).

In the rest of this chapter, we will consider the seals, trumpets and bowl judgements in this context and omit most of the parenthetic passages.

A. The Seal Judgements.

The First Seal - Revelation 6:1-2.

Then I saw when the Lamb broke one of the seven seals, and I heard one of the four living creatures saying, as with a voice of thunder, "Come". I looked and behold a white horse, and he who sat on it had a bow; and a crown was given to him, and he went out conquering and to conquer.

Here we have a person riding a white horse, a bow in his hand, and wearing a crown. We are also told that he went forth 'conquering and to conquer' (v.2).

These verses describe the rise of the Antichrist and his warfare at the beginning of the seven years of the tribulation. We know it is not Christ who is described here because the rider is seen wearing a 'staphanos' crown, which is the crown of an overcomer or victor, whereas Christ will wear the 'diadem' crown, the crown of sovereignty and royalty.

From our studies previously in Daniel we know that the Antichrist arises through overcoming three of the ten existing world rulers (Daniel 7:8). It is this event which commences the seven seals.

We can see the effects of the rise of this Antichrist from the pattern of the next five seals.

The Second Seal - Revelation 6:3-4.

When he broke the second seal, I heard the second living creature saying, "Come." And another, a red horse, went out; and to him who sat on it, it was granted to take peace from the earth, and that men would slay one another; and a great sword was given him.

With the second horseman of the Apocalypse, peace is removed from the earth. This will be the natural result of the Antichrist going forth to conquer. The sword is the general symbol of war, bloodshed, and national civil strife.

There are three wars during the Tribulation period and the second seal is the first of these. The second major war is in the middle of the Tribulation and the third, which is the Campaign of Armageddon, at the end of the Tribulation.

The Third Seal - Revelation 6:5-6.

When he broke the third seal, I heard the third living creature saying "Come." I looked, and behold, a black horse; and he who sat on it had a pair of scales in his hand. And I heard something like a voice in the centre of the four living creatures saying, "A quart of wheat for a denarius, and three quarts of barley for a denarius; and do not damage the oil and wine."

We have read of a white horse, a red horse, and now we have a black horse and rider. This rider has a pair of balances in his hand for the weighing out of food. Following the war, we now have a famine on the earth. Even in our own lifetime we have seen this very thing in various countries following civil wars. War draws men from the land and prevents them from sowing and harvesting (e.g. the Ethiopian crisis of the mid-1980s).

A denarius was a daily wage and a quart of corn a slave's daily ration which could normally be purchased for one-eighth of a denarius. In normal times one could buy eight measures of wheat or twenty-four measures of barley for a denarius. In these verses food is eight times the normal price.

Judgement however is tempered with mercy in the instruction, 'do not damage the oil and wine'. These items were used for medicinal purposes.

The Fourth Seal - Revelation 6:7-8.

When the Lamb broke the fourth seal, I heard the voice of the fourth living creature saying, "come." I looked and behold an ashen horse; and he who sat on it had the name Death; and Hades was following with him. Authority was given to them over a fourth of the earth, to kill with sword and with famine and with pestilence and by the wild beasts of the earth.

The fourth horseman of the Apocalypse is the deadliest of all. Death and Hades are here personified. The action of these destroys one fourth of the world's population. It could be by the sword, (perhaps another war), famine, pestilence and disease, and the attacks of wild beasts.

Please note, 28 Million died of influenza after First World War. It could be that following this end time war, a similar phenomenon occurs.

The Fifth Seal - Revelation 6:9-11.

When the Lamb broke the fifth seal, I saw underneath the altar the souls of those who had been slain because of the word of God, and because of the testimony which they had maintained; and they cried out with a loud voice, saying, "How long, O Lord, holy and true, will You refrain from judging and avenging our blood on those who dwell on the earth?" And there was given to each of them a white robe; and they were told that they should rest for a little while longer, until the number of their fellow servants and their brethren who were to be killed even as they had been, would be completed also.

The fifth seal deals with the Christian martyrs during the Tribulation. There is a cry from these martyrs for justice and the promise is made that justice will be given to them once the full number of martyrs has been completed.

Revelation 17:6 tells us that the persecutor is ecclesiastical Babylon. Again, we will develop this theme in chapter 12.

The Sixth Seal - Revelation 6:12-17.

I looked when He broke the sixth seal, and there was a great earthquake; and the sun became black as sackcloth made of hair, and the whole moon became like blood; and the stars of the sky fell to the earth, as a fig tree casts its unripe figs when shaken by a great wind. The sky was split apart like a scroll when it is rolled up, and every mountain and island were moved out of their places. Then the kings of the earth and the great men and the commanders and the rich and the strong and every slave and free man hid themselves in the caves and among the rocks of the mountains; and they said to the mountains and to the rocks, "Fall on us and hide us from the presence of Him who sits on the throne, and from the wrath of the Lamb; for the great day of their wrath has come, and who is able to stand?"

As a result of the opening of this seal we have the wrath of God revealed directly for the first time. In contrast with this, the first five seals are all natural results of the rise of the Antichrist and the persecution of God's people. There are seven results from this sixth seal.

i. A great earthquake. This is the first of five earthquakes in Revelation (Revelation 6:12; 8:5; 11:13, 11:19, and 16:17-21, (cf. Zechariah 14:4-8)).
ii. The sun became black as sackcloth made of hair. Three times in Bible history this has taken place: Genesis 1:2; Exodus 10:21-23; Matthew 27:45. Five times during the Tribulation the sun will be darkened: Revelation 6:12; 8:12; 9:2; 16:10; Matthew 24:29.
iii. The moon became as blood corresponding to the darkening of the sun.
iv. The stars fell to the earth. These will not be planets or the sun, but meteors.
v. The sky receded, or split apart as a scroll. It will not pass out of existence but will be terribly affected by what God is doing on the earth.
vi. And every mountain and island was moved out of its place. Again, they do not pass away but are rocked by the cataclysmic events.
vii. The great day of wrath is come. Anarchy ensues as men try to escape from the wrath of God.

The Seventh Seal - Revelation 8:1-6.

> *When the Lamb broke the seventh seal, there was silence in heaven for about half an hour. And I saw the seven angels who stand before God, and seven trumpets were given to them. Another angel came and stood at the altar, holding a golden censer; and much incense was given to him, so that he might add it to the prayers of all the saints on the golden altar which was before the throne. And the smoke of the incense, with the prayers of the saints, went up before God out of the angel's hand. Then the angel took the censer and filled it with the fire of the altar, and threw it to the earth; and there followed peals of thunder and sounds and flashes of lightning and an earthquake. And the seven angels who had the seven trumpets prepared themselves to sound them.*

The Seventh seal, when opened, is an explanation to what is happening in heaven prior to the sounding of the trumpet judgements. After a period of silence the seven angels are given their trumpets to sound, and then an angel ministers at the golden alter with a censer of incense. Who this angel is, we are not told, but it could be the Lord Jesus Christ, himself. In the Old Testament, only the High Priest could carry out this administration, so it could be that in heaven our Great High Priest is also doing this, and lifting the prayers of the saints to God.

As the prayers of the saints in Revelation 6:9-11 have risen before the throne during this seventh seal, so the judgements coming upon the earth by the angelic trumpets are God's answer to the martyr's requests (6:10).

B. The Trumpet Judgements.

The First Trumpet - Revelation 8:7.

The first sounded, and there came hail and fire, mixed with blood, and they were thrown to the earth; and a third of the earth was burned up, and a third of the trees were burned up, and all the green grass was burned up.

As has been said previously, there is no reason why these trumpet judgements should not be taken literally, unless the context suggests otherwise.

With the sounding of this first trumpet a third of the earth's surface vegetation is destroyed, maybe burned up as a result of a meteorite shower.

The Second Trumpet - Revelation 8:8-9.

The second angel sounded, and something like a great mountain burning with fire was thrown into the sea; and a third of the sea became blood, and a third of the creatures which were in the sea and had life, died; and a third of the ships were destroyed.

The great mountain burning with fire may refer to a meteor or a volcano, but the results are supernatural, for they of themselves could not turn the sea to blood. Some of these judgements are similar to those that God brought upon Egypt.

Only one third of the sea and creatures will be affected, but the fishing business of the world will be crippled (this is particularly relevant in the Mediterranean) and men will begin to recognise that these judgements are from God.

The Third Trumpet - Revelation 8:10-11.

> *The third angel sounded, and a great star fell from heaven, burning like a torch, and it fell on a third of the rivers and on the springs of waters. The name of the star is called Wormwood; and a third of the waters became wormwood, and many men died from the waters, because they were made bitter.*

This could be another meteor whose gaseous vapours will poison the rivers and mountains. Alternatively, whenever the word star is used symbolically, it is always a symbol of an angel. The angel's name is Wormwood, showing the angel to be a fallen one. This angel causes one third of the sweet water to turn bitter which in turn causes the death of many.

God will use fallen angels on occasions to bring judgement upon the earth.

The Fourth Trumpet - Revelation 8:12.

> *The fourth angel sounded, and a third of the sun and a third of the moon and a third of the stars were struck, so that a third of them would be darkened and the day would not shine for a third of it, and the night in the same way.*

Here the light sources from the heavenly bodies are somehow hindered so that the earth only receives two thirds of its normal light.

The Three Woes (Parenthesis) Revelation 8:13

> *Then I looked, and I heard an eagle flying in mid-heaven, saying with a loud voice, "Woe, woe, woe to those who dwell on the earth, because of the remaining blasts of the trumpet of the three angels who are about to sound!"*

Clearly, the angels in heaven are deeply moved as they look upon the destruction of God's creation through these judgements, however, they also declare that even worse is about to befall the earth.

The three woes of the last three trumpets are:

1. The plague of demon locusts out of the abyss, 9:1-12.
2. The plague of demon horsemen out of the abyss, 9:13-21.
3. The judgement of the nations 11:15-19.

The Fifth Trumpet: The First Woe - Revelation 9:1-12.

Then the fifth angel sounded, and I saw a star from heaven which had fallen to the earth; and the key of the bottomless pit was given to him. He opened the bottomless pit, and smoke went up out of the pit, like the smoke of a great furnace; and the sun and the air were darkened by the smoke of the pit. Then out of the smoke came locusts upon the earth, and power was given them, as the scorpions of the earth have power. They were told not to hurt the grass of the earth, nor any green thing, nor any tree, but only the men who do not have the seal of God on their foreheads. And they were not permitted to kill anyone, but to torment for five months; and their torment was like the torment of a scorpion when it stings a man. And in those days men will seek death and will not find it; they will long to die, and death flees from them.

The appearance of the locusts was like horses prepared for battle; and on their heads appeared to be crowns like gold, and their faces were like the faces of men. They had hair like the hair of women, and their teeth were like the teeth of lions. They had breastplates like breastplates of iron; and the sound of their wings was like the sound of chariots, of many horses rushing to battle. They have tails like scorpions, and stings; and in their tails is their power to hurt men for five months. They have as king over them, the angel of the abyss; his name in Hebrew is Abaddon, and in the Greek he has the name Apollyon. The first woe is past; behold, two woes are still coming after these things.

We now enter a new phase of judgements. The first four have affected the material creation, but the last three affect the moral creation. The fact that they are called 'woes' intimates their severity.

We are told that a star fallen from heaven is, in fact, an angel, similar to 'Wormwood' who was unleashed as a result of the third trumpet blast, and he opens the bottomless pit where fallen angels are confined. When the abyss is opened the third blackout occurs by this cloud of angels issuing forth.

This is the first of two demonic invasions within the End Times. These demons are commanded not to destroy the vegetation but only to torment people who do not have the seal of God on their foreheads (Jews and/or believers).

They are to kill no one, but only torment them for five months. Not only will the demons be unable to kill but also the tormented persons, even should they want to die, will not be able to do so. They will even find suicide impossible to carry out.

The leader of this demonic hoard is named Abaddon, or Apollyon. Both words mean 'destruction.'

The Sixth Trumpet: The Second Woe - Revelation 9:13-21.

> *Then the sixth angel sounded, and I heard a voice from the four horns of the golden altar which is before God, one saying to the sixth angel who had the trumpet, "Release the four angels who are bound at the great river Euphrates." And the four angels, who had been prepared for the hour and day and month and year, were released, so that they would kill a third of mankind. The number of the armies of the horsemen was two hundred million; I heard the number of them. And this is how I saw in the vision the horses and those who sat on them: the riders had breastplates the colour of fire and of hyacinth and of brimstone; and the heads of the horses are like the heads of lions; and out of their mouths proceed fire and smoke and brimstone. A third of mankind was killed by these three plagues, by the fire and the smoke and the brimstone which proceeded out of their mouths. For the power of the horses is in their mouths and in their tails; for their tails are like serpents and have heads, and with them they do harm.*
>
> *The rest of mankind, who were not killed by these plagues, did not repent of the works of their hands, so as not to worship demons, and the idols of gold and of silver and of brass and of stone and of wood, which can neither see nor hear nor walk; and they did not repent of their murders nor of their sorceries nor of their immorality nor of their thefts.*

Now four angels who had been bound at the Euphrates River are released and these are the leaders of the second demonic invasion. Under the fifth trumpet the demons were instructed not to kill whereas these demons are told to kill one third of mankind.

The number of demons in this second invasion is numbered at 200 million and they bring death by plague of some sort. Yet for all these, men do not repent, but continue to worship other gods and involve themselves in the occult.

The Seventh Trumpet: The Third Woe - Revelation 11:14-19.

The second woe is past; behold, the third woe is coming quickly.

Then the seventh angel sounded; and there were loud voices in heaven, saying, "The Kingdom of the world has become the Kingdom of our Lord and of His Christ; and He will reign forever and ever." And the twenty-four elders, who sit on their thrones before God, fell on their faces and worshiped God, saying, "We give You thanks, O Lord God, the Almighty, who are and who were, because You have taken Your great power and have begun to reign. "And the nations were enraged, and Your wrath came, and the time came for the dead to be judged, and the time to reward Your bond-servants the prophets and the saints and those who fear Your name, the small and the great, and to destroy those who destroy the earth." And the temple of God which is in heaven was opened; and the ark of His covenant appeared in His temple, and there were flashes of lightning and sounds and peals of thunder and an earthquake and a great hailstorm.

This trumpet announces that Christ will inherit the Kingdom of the world, and that He will come with fierce wrath upon all who follow the Unholy Trinity of the Antichrist, the False Prophet and Satan. This is followed by upheavals in the earth and violent storms.

In addition, at this point, the final events of the End Times are summarised: the judgement of the dead and the reward of the righteous.

C. The Bowl Judgements.

The bowl judgements are the final outpouring of God's wrath upon the earth (15:1). Since the last trumpet ended with the return of Christ, these bowl judgements occur either during the time between the sixth and seventh trumpet or between the conclusion of the judgement announced by the seventh trumpet and the return of Christ. These judgements are delivered by the hands of seven angels who come forth from the temple of God in heaven (16:1).

The First Bowl Judgement - Revelation 16:2.

So the first angel went and poured out his bowl on the earth; and it became a loathsome and malignant sore on the people who had the mark of the beast and who worshiped his image.

The first judgement results in horrible sores, or perhaps skin ulcers or boils breaking out upon all those who have the mark of the beast and worship his image.

The Second Bowl Judgement - Revelation 16:3.

The second angel poured out his bowl into the sea, and it became blood like that of a dead man; and every living thing in the sea died.

Under the second trumpet Judgement, all of the sea is affected. Since the salt water will be turned into blood, this will destroy all remaining sea life (c.f. Revelation 8:8-9 where one third of sea life has already been destroyed).

The Third Bowl Judgement - Revelation 16:4-7.

Then the third angel poured out his bowl into the rivers and the springs of waters; and they became blood.

Again, under the third trumpet judgement, the fresh water is destroyed - the water in rivers and springs becomes blood.

The angel declares the unswerving justice of God. Since men have shed the blood of the prophets and saints, mankind is given blood to drink and so in verse 7 another angel affirms God's righteous judgements.

The Fourth Bowl Judgement - Revelation 16:8-9.

The fourth angel poured out his bowl upon the sun, and it was given to it to scorch men with fire. Men were scorched with fierce heat; and they blasphemed the name of God who has the power over these plagues, and they did not repent so as to give Him glory.

Whereas the fourth trumpet judgement affected the sun by destroying one third of the light source, the fourth bowl will affect the sun, by increasing its temperature to the point where men are totally scorched.

Mankind will recognise the source of this judgement as coming from God but instead of turning to Him in faith, they will blaspheme His name.

The Fifth Bowl Judgement - Revelation 16:10-11.

Then the fifth angel poured out his bowl on the throne of the beast, and his Kingdom became darkened; and they gnawed their tongues because of pain, and they blasphemed the God of heaven because of their pains and their sores; and they did not repent of their deeds.

Among the various results of the fifth trumpet judgement is another blackout. The fifth bowl judgement will result in the fourth blackout of the End Times. The entire Kingdom of the Antichrist will be darkened, which, at this stage will include the entire world.

Along with the darkness comes a gnawing pain that will cause mankind to blaspheme all the more.

The Sixth Bowl Judgement - Revelation 16:12-16.

The sixth angel poured out his bowl on the great river, the Euphrates; and its water was dried up, so that the way would be prepared for the kings from the east. And I saw coming out of the mouth of the dragon and out of the mouth of the beast and out of the mouth of the false prophet, three unclean spirits like frogs; for they are spirits of demons, performing signs, which go out to the kings of the whole world, to gather them together for the war of the great day of God, the Almighty. ("Behold, I am coming like a thief Blessed is the one who stays awake and keeps his clothes, so that he will not walk about naked and men will not see his shame.") And they gathered them together to the place which in Hebrew is called Har-Magedon.

This judgement begins with the assembling of the allies of the Antichrist to come to the Battle of Armageddon. The purpose of drying up the Euphrates will be for the assembly of the Antichrist's Babylonian forces. This is in accordance with God's purposes (see Zephaniah 3:8) who will gather the armies of the world in order to bring his judgement upon them.

All three members of the counterfeit trinity are involved in this campaign against the Jews, and they have sent out demon messengers to call to battle, by miraculous signs, the seven kings who are under the authority of the Antichrist.

Between the sixth and seventh bowl judgements the battle takes place with the defeat of the Antichrist and his forces. At the end of the battle, the Lord Jesus Christ comes to earth, and a voice cries out, "It is finished," v.17.

The Seventh Bowl Judgement - Revelation 16:17-21.

> *Then the seventh angel poured out his bowl upon the air, and a loud voice came out of the temple from the throne, saying, "It is done." And there were flashes of lightning and sounds and peals of thunder; and there was a great earthquake, such as there had not been since man came to be upon the earth, so great an earthquake was it, and so mighty. The great city was split into three parts, and the cities of the nations fell Babylon the great was remembered before God, to give her the cup of the wine of His fierce wrath. And every island fled away, and the mountains were not found. And huge hailstones, about one hundred pounds each, came down from heaven upon men; and men blasphemed God because of the plague of the hail, because its plague was extremely severe.*

The seventh bowl brings the Tribulation to an end, and the earthquake which comes with this bowl judgement will cause the city of Jerusalem to split into three divisions, while the city of Babylon will suffer the full wrath of God, (v.19).

Many geographical changes will take place and hail will fall weighing approximately 100lbs. This earthquake that will shake Jerusalem is further described in Zechariah 14:4-5.

Not only will Jerusalem be split into three divisions, but also the Mount of Olives will be split into two parts creating a valley running east to west.

The Great Tribulation will come to an end with these cataclysmic events.

Chapter 12

Revelation III: The Two Witnesses, the Unholy Trinity and Babylon the Great

Introduction

In revelation, a number of characters emerge during the course of the narrative who play a principle role during the Great Tribulation. In this chapter we will examine some of these characters and seek to gain an understanding of them and their part in the End Times.

The Two Witnesses

In Revelation 11, two characters appear whom God declares are 'My two witnesses'. They appear during the final phase of the reign of the Antichrist and their role appears to be to 'prophesy' on the earth, or to speak God's message to the world. They also have power to unleash some of the judgements which come upon the earth as a result of the sounding of the seven trumpets and the pouring out of the bowls (see chapter 11 above).

Revelation 11 verse 4 tells us that, 'These are the two olive trees and the two lampstands that stand before the Lord of the earth' (C.f. Zechariah

4.14 'the two anointed ones', filled with God's spirit).

As to the identity of these two we are given no clear indication. Previously in chapter 7 we said that they are typified by Zerubbabel and Joshua (see Zechariah 4). Thus, they represent civil authority and priestly authority. Some have speculated that they are Moses and Elijah representing the law and the prophets (see the transfiguration). Alternatively they are just two witnesses whom God is saving to stand against the Antichrist during the End Times. They may even be two symbolic characters who represent godly leadership who will stand against the Antichrist for this period. We cannot know for certain but what we do know is that they are sent from God.

In Revelation 11:3 we are told that they will 'Prophesy for 1260 days' (3 years, 165 days). This is during the second part of the Tribulation because, following their demise, comes the blast of the seventh trumpet which concludes with the commencement of the reign of Jesus Christ himself.

Tremendous power and authority are given to these witnesses, even to the controlling of the weather (v.6) and over the elements of the earth. Ultimately, the Antichrist kills them (v.7) and they are left to lie in the streets of Jerusalem (v.8) for 3 ½ days.

In verse 10 we are told that the people of the world are unrepentant, despite the testimony of the Two Witnesses. But in verse 11 we see that God will raise them from the dead.

Including the extra 3 days, this brings their time on earth to exactly 3 years and 24 weeks. Immediately following these events, Christ will return (Revelation 11:15-19).

The Unholy Trinity

The Unholy Trinity is the name given to the three principle proponents of evil during the End times. We see the Unholy Trinity revealed in Revelation chapters 12 to 13. Let us examine each of them in turn.

The Dragon, the Beast from the Sea, and the Beast from the Earth

The Dragon

We saw in Chapter 7 how Revelation 12:3 represents Satan and his activities in the final seven years of history – how he will:

- Persecute the Jews
- Persecute the remaining Christians
- Energize the Antichrist
- Obtain worship from the inhabitants of the earth through the Antichrist

This period will be the last attempt of Satan to destroy God's creation and thwart God's plan to bring all things back under subjection to His authority. It begins when Satan is finally thrown out of heaven (his current residence (see Ephesians 6:12)), and is confined to the earth. At this point, all hell begins to break out on earth during the Tribulation.

Satan will seek to work out his rule upon the earth via the Antichrist (his own spawn), until he is defeated and dealt with at the return of Christ.

The ultimate doom of Satan is dealt with in Revelation 20:1-10. There we see him bound in chains and thrown into the abyss (a place prepared for him to hold him pending ultimate judgement). In Revelation 20:7, we see him released from the abyss once more and allowed to deceive the earth again. It is difficult to understand why God will allow this. Certainly, this period of the future is shrouded in mystery, and we are only given snatches of revelation concerning this time such as in this passage.

Finally, Satan will be thrown into the lake of fire where he will remain forever (Revelation 20:10).

The Beast from the Sea

The beast from the sea is the Antichrist and the Kingdom over which he rules – the two are interchangeable (as we have seen from our studies in Daniel). See Chapter 6 & 7 for more detail concerning this member of the Unholy Trinity.

During the Tribulation he will be the world leader, however, his reign will be brought to an end when the Messiah returns.

As to the number of the Beast himself (Revelation 13:18 - 666), many people have postulated different notions concerning what this might mean. Suffice to say, those alive at the end will recognise it.

The doom of the Antichrist is dealt with in Revelation 19:20-21, where we see him thrown into the lake of fire – the place reserved for eternal judgement (Hell).

The Beast from the Earth

The beast from the earth is the False Prophet who works alongside the Antichrist during the Tribulation to reinforce his rule. It is this character who will act on behalf of the Antichrist. Maybe he will be a government minister (v.12). Certainly, the work of propaganda rests with him (v.14, cf. 19:20). Somehow, in supernatural power, he will cause the Antichrist's image, which will be set up in the Temple (the 'abomination of desolation'), to come to life or at least to speak and proclaim judgements on behalf of the Antichrist. Taken literally, this would be an amazing phenomenon which would have the power to deceive; if we take it figuratively, it may be some kind of device (yet to be invented) which is based in the Temple through which 'justice' is dispensed on behalf of the regime of the Antichrist, and which enables the end time residents of the earth to trade. Certainly the notion of a mark of recognition or identification (v.16-17) would support this view.

The False Prophet will also end up in the lake of fire at the return of Christ (Revelation 19:20-21, 20:10).

Babylon the Great

Isaiah makes a number of references to Babylon and it is here that we start to see her symbolic significance; Barry Webb[39] makes the following statement, commenting on Isaiah 47:

'...Babylon here is not merely the ancient city of that name...Like Jerusalem with which it is contrasted, it is both a concrete historical reality and a symbol and it is the symbolic significance of Babylon which is primary here....The sin of Babylon is not simply its pride and self absorption, but its self-deification (c.f. Isaiah 14:12-14). The twice uttered I am, and there is none besides me (8, 10), is a direct challenge to the Lord's identical claim in (Isaiah) 45:5, and this defiance of God finds concrete expression in abuse of his people (v.6). As in (Isaiah) 14:3-23, Babylon represents humankind organised in defiance of God – the Kingdom of mere mortals, in contrast to the Kingdom of God. In this

[39] *Barry Webb in The Message of Isaiah (Leicester: IVP, 2003) p.190*

sense, Babylon is still with us, and still stands under the judgement of God. The historical Babylon of the sixth century BC was merely one manifestation of it.'

We first encounter the harlot, Babylon, in Zechariah 5:5-11. In this passage, she is revealed as taking the Ephah (container for measuring grain used in trade) to Shinar (Babylon) to build a temple for herself where she will sit 'on her own pedestal'.

In Revelation 17 and 18 her doom is explained in detail and here we see some of the characteristics that identify for us who she is. However, before we examine these, we must first consider the role of Babylon throughout scripture. At strategic points in history Babylon arises and is a symbol of Man's rebellion or self-exaltation.

In Genesis 9:20-27, we see the curse which came upon Ham as a result of exposing his father's folly to all and sundry. It is from this cursed line that we see the appearance of Nimrod. The story of Nimrod is detailed in the ancient epic of Gilgamesh. From Genesis 10:6-12, we know that:

His name, Nimrod, means Rebel, and that he was a 'Mighty hunter against the lord' (this is often mistranslated 'before the Lord'). We also know that he established cities (Babel, Erech, Accad and Calneh in Babylonia and a whole list of cities in Assyria including Nineveh. Symbolically, cities are places established for protection i.e. self preservation as opposed to trusting in God).

In Genesis 11:1-9 we see the Tower of Babel established. Most scholars agree that this was probably some kind of ziggurat built for worship of the stars, hence its height meant that the stars could be seen more clearly (11:4) – astrology has its roots in Babylon and continues to be followed by the Zoroastrians who still live in Iraq. On the ancient site of Babylon, the foundations of an ancient ziggurat have been identified which could have been the Tower of Babel.

- The purpose of the Tower was:
- To dispense with God (they were building their own way to Heaven)
- To glorify man ('let us make a name for ourselves' – Genesis 11:4)
- To seek of the stars more easily (astrology)

The dynamics of the people who built the tower were that that they were:

- United by a common language
- United by a common purpose – rebellion against God

In response to their rebellion, God:

- Confused their languages
- Scattered them across the whole earth so that they would not continue to be united in rebellion against Him

The characteristics of these people were the same characteristics which will typify the End Time people of the world. They will:

- Be fully rebellious – anti-God, anti-Christ
- Be independent of God (Evolution, Communism)
- Glorify man (Humanism)
- Seek a United World Government

Again the qualities of the society of the ancient people of Babylon can be likened to those of the End Times and are typified by,

- Military Power
- Wealth & Prosperity (Worldly Economics)
- Glorifying of human wisdom (Psychology)
- A blasphemous religious system (Idolatry)

Ishtar (Asherah, Astarte, Isis), Queen of Heaven

A key goddess in the Babylonian pantheon was Ishtar who was entitled 'the Queen of Heaven' (Revelation 18:7). Details about her include the following:

- She was the wife or consort or associate of Bel (Marduk, Osiris, Baal).
- She was portrayed naked, riding on a horse or a lion with a serpent (Revelation 17:3).
- Her cult included male prostitution, orgies, murder, etc.
- She was the goddess of sensual love, maternity and fertility. She

was also a hunting goddess.
- She claimed that she had conceived from heaven.
- She went into the forest and was killed by wild animals, and was raised from the dead.
- Most heathen religions include this image, which has its roots in her.
- She is the mother of witchcraft (Isis, Astarte).

She sums up the image of Babylon (see below) and it is these characteristics which will typify the end time world system which will be destroyed at the return of Christ.

In Jeremiah 51:1-10, we see the destruction of Babylon prophesied. Whilst these prophecies primarily relate to the literal destruction of the city of Babylon in BC536, the language used is repeated in the Revelation passage and will be fulfilled upon the end time Babylon.

Revelation 17 - 18

In Revelation 17 to 18, we see the following characteristics:

- She rides on the back of the Beast (17:3). In other words, her prominence and power are attributed to her because of her relationship with the final world empire.
- She sits on many waters (17:1) which verse 15 tells us are the inhabitants of the whole world.
- She seduces the 'kings of the earth'.
- She 'drinks the blood of the saints'. In other words, the persecution of the Church during the End Times is as a result of her direct actions.
- She is identified as 'the great city which reigns over the kings of the earth'. We will explore this notion below.

Who is She?

She combines 2 elements: religious authority and economic authority. She leads the kings of the earth in immorality and at her demise the merchants weep (18:11-20).

Some have postulated that she is the established church (the Church of Rome) which the Antichrist will use and then destroy, or she may be all of the false religious systems put together. She is also the economic systems which are now universal and which are used to control the world. We live in a single world economy, the collapse of which will come in the End Times and will cause much wealth to be lost and hence the merchants cry.

Ultimately Satan's desire is worship of himself. He will use the religious systems as a vehicle to establish that and he will use the economic systems to control the earth prior to their complete destruction.

In the end, as Satan will become desperate, and as the war reaches its climax, all the systems of control built up on this earth will come crashing down and finally, Satan himself will be defeated before the Lamb of God.

Summary

In these chapters, we have considered the book of Revelation up to chapter 19 in some detail. We will return to Revelation in Chapter 15 as we deal with the end time judgements and the new heavens and the new earth.

Suffice to say, Revelation gives a detailed insight into the events of the Tribulation culminating in the return of Christ, demonstrating that this period will be a time of awful destruction and devastation which will culminate in the completion of God's wrath poured out on the earth.

Section 3

The Teaching of the New Testament

Chapter 13

The End Times in the Gospels

Introduction

Over the years, many people have used the parables of Jesus to build doctrines concerning the End Times, such as the Triumphant Church based on scriptures such as the Parable of the Wheat and the Tares. Whilst acknowledging that 'all scripture is inspired by God and profitable for teaching, for reproof, for correction, for training in righteousness' (2 Timothy 3:16), when building doctrine our starting point must be the clear teaching of scripture. Illustrations and imagery must then be fitted into that which scripture states explicitly.

Thus, the focus of this chapter will be the clear teaching of Jesus in the Gospels.

Matthew 24 & 25, Luke 17: 22-37, 21:10-36, Mark 13: 1-37

Jesus' teaching concerning the End Times is given largely during the days between his triumphal entry into Jerusalem and his trial and crucifixion. We find this teaching in the above passages. For the purpose of this chapter, we will use Matthew 24 and 25 as our base passage, and will refer to the other parallel passages only as they add more information.

Matthew 24 commences with the disciples admiring the temple buildings and, starting with the destruction of the Temple itself, Jesus begins to open up the future to them.

In verse 2, he refers to the destruction of the Temple which was to occur in AD 70. The disciples broaden the discussion by asking about 'the sign of your coming and the end of the age'. Clearly, the disciples had an understanding that the coming of Jesus in Messianic power was somehow tied in with the End Times. Jesus responds by informing them of some of the things which will occur prior to His coming which are not signs of the end:

- False Christ's will arise (v.5) and will mislead some.
- There will be wars and rumours of wars (v.6).
- Nation will rise against nation and Kingdom against Kingdom (v.7).
- There will be famines and earthquakes (v.7).

Jesus states clearly 'these things must take place but that is not the end…these things are merely the beginning of birth pangs' Luke adds emphasis to this with the words 'but the end does not follow immediately.' (Luke 21:9). All of these things have occurred frequently in the last two thousand years and are signs that we are in the last phase of human history but that we are not yet in the last days.

However, Jesus goes onto say, 'then they will deliver you to tribulation…' (v.9). At this point there is a transition in the narrative and Jesus moves on to describe the last days. This passage is directed towards the disciples and therefore is specifically talking to those who are the followers of Jesus. They will be:

- Delivered to tribulation (v.9, cf. Mark 13:9, Luke 21:16)
- Hated by all nations because of My name (v.9 the name of Jesus – cf. Mark 13:13, Luke 21:17)
- Many will fall away and betray one another (v.10 cf. Mark 13:12)
- Many false prophets will arise and will mislead many (v.11)
- Most people's love will grow cold because of lawlessness (v.12)
- The gospel of the Kingdom will be preached to the whole world as a testimony to all the nations (v. 14, c.f. Mark 13:10)

It is this last event that ushers in the end (c.f. Revelation 10:7, 15-19).

Next, Jesus turns to another event which, from our studies in Daniel, we know will occur halfway through the Tribulation: the setting up of the idolatrous image of the Antichrist in the Temple (v.15-21). Luke gives us a slightly different perspective on this with the words 'when you see Jerusalem surrounded by armies then recognise that her desolation is near' (Luke 21:20). We also know that the injunction to flee during these days is specific to the nation of Israel (Luke 21:23 'wrath to this people', c.f. Revelation 12:13). Mark (Mark 13:14) specifically tells us that this refers to 'those in Judea'. However, we also know that on the failure of Satan to destroy Israel, his attention will turn to the persecution of the Christians alive at that time (Revelation 12:17). Hence, Jesus says that 'for the sake of the elect those days will be cut short' (v.22).

In verses 23 to 26 of Matthew 24, Jesus picks up the theme once more of false prophets and false Christ's arising to deceive even the Christians alive at his coming. The injunction to his listeners is not to believe such people, since the coming of Jesus ('The Son of Man' (v.27), c.f. Daniel 7:13), will be clear to all like a flash of lightning in the sky.

In verses 29 to 31, Jesus lays out for us the actual events which will occur at His coming 'immediately after the Tribulation' (i.e. at the end of the last seven years):

- the sun will be darkened (v.29)
- the moon will not give its light (v.29)
- the stars will fall from the sky (v.29)
- the powers of the heavens (the spiritual principalities (see Ephesians 6: 12)) will be shaken (v.29)
- the sign of the Son of Man will appear in the sky (v.30). We do not know what this sign is but from the context (cf. v.27) it will be clear to all
- the tribes of the earth will mourn (v.30, i.e. all nations)
- they will all see his coming (v. 30, c.f. Daniel 7:13)

It is at this point, when His coming is seen by all, that he will gather together His elect in what is known as the Rapture (v.31). Mark adds that they will be gathered 'from the farthest ends of the earth to the farthest end of heaven' (Mark 13: 27). In other words, the Rapture includes the living and the dead who are 'the elect' (see. 1 Corinthians

15:51-52, 1 Thessalonians 4:16-17).

The message of verses 32 to 35 is that the listeners will be able to recognise these events and will thereby know that Jesus is about to come. He goes on to affirm that His words are accurate, trustworthy and reliable (v.34-35).

In verses 36 to 41, Jesus emphasises that for those who are not watching for these signs, these things will come as a surprise, just as the flood came to those who had ignored Noah's warnings. It is in this way that the Rapture will surprise those who are not expecting Jesus' return (v.40-41). Luke (Luke 17: 28-32) adds the example of the days of Lot, where people in Sodom were carrying on their daily lives as normal right up until the time when judgement fell upon them.

In the final section of this chapter, Jesus gives a warning to His followers to be on the alert (notice the term used 'your Lord' in v.42). This theme continues through the following two parables: the Parable of the Wise and Foolish Virgins, and the Parable of the Talents. In both parables, the emphasis is on being ready, prepared, alert and in faithful service at the time of His coming. What is also emphasised (24:51, 25:12, 25:30) is that judgement of some sort will fall upon those who are His servants but who are found misbehaving (24:29), unprepared (25:8), or wasting their talents and opportunities (25:26-27) at His coming. It is not my purpose in this book to discuss the assurance of salvation or the meaning of this judgement specifically. Suffice to say, the injunction of Jesus is for His people to be ready and watchful. This same theme is picked up in 1 Thessalonians 5:1-11.

Finally, in Matthew 25:31-46, Jesus introduces the Judgement of the Nations at His coming. This passage is not to do with judgement of the righteous and unrighteous per se. Rather, it is a specific judgement concerning how the nations have treated 'these brothers of mine'. We have three options concerning who these 'brothers' are:

- The physical brothers of Jesus, i.e. the Jews
- The spiritual brothers of Jesus, i.e. the Church
- Those whom Jesus identifies as brothers, i.e. the downtrodden (the hungry, thirsty, strangers, naked, sick, and imprisoned)

Of these options, the first accords most consistently with scripture (Joel 3:1-17, Zechariah 14:1-8, etc.). The judgement upon the nations is not simply for how they have treated (or mistreated) the Jews but also how they have neglected to care for them despite the dispersion.

For further detail on this judgement, refer to chapter 9.

John

In contrast with the synoptic gospels, the gospel of John does not contain a great deal of specific teaching concerning the End Times, but makes reference to it in passing when relating the teaching of Jesus on other specific subjects. The first of these is in John 5:25 to 31 where Jesus makes reference to the Resurrection. In this passage we see that:

- The dead will be resurrected when they hear Jesus' voice (v.25)
- Jesus has authority to execute judgement (v.27)
- All the dead will be raised (v.29)
    - The good to resurrection life
    - The evil to a resurrection of judgement

The Resurrection of the dead and the fact that Christ will preside over the judgement is reaffirmed in the following verses: 6:39, 40, 44, and 54 and in 12:48.

In John 14:1-5, Jesus affirms that he is the only way to the Father. In doing so he also indicates two truths regarding the future:

- He has gone to prepare a place for his disciples (all who believe in Him)
- He will come again and receive his disciples to himself so that they can be with him

Summary

From the teachings contained within the gospels, we can be sure that

- Jesus will return to this earth
- His coming will be unexpected by the world
- His people need to be on the alert pending his return
- The time just prior to his return will include tribulation for his people, both Jews and Christians
- His coming will be in judgement

Chapter 14

The End Times in the New Testament Epistles

Introduction

Throughout the letters of Paul to various churches, frequent reference is made to living with an expectation of the coming of the Lord and of future glory (e.g. Romans 8:18). However, in this section we will focus on passages where Paul gives specific teaching to the churches, either in response to questions, or in order to ensure that they are not ignorant on these subjects. In addition, we will look at references to the End Times in the letters of Peter and Jude.

1 Corinthians 15

In 1 Corinthians 15, Paul deals with the subject of the resurrection, not only of Christ, but of those who have died. What makes this passage worthy of study in regard to the End Times is that he positions this latter event as happening concurrently with the return of Christ. Having argued that '...if there is no resurrection of the dead, not even Christ has been raised, and if Christ has not been raised, then our preaching is vain, your faith is also vain' (1 Corinthians 15 13-14), he goes on to establish the order of the Resurrection.

> *For as in Adam all die, so also in Christ all will be made alive. But each in his own order: Christ the first fruits, after that those who are Christ's at His coming, then comes the end, when he hands over the Kingdom to the God and Father , when He has abolished all rule and authority and power. For He must reign until he has put all His enemies under his feet (1 Corinthians 15: 22-25).*

Thus, Paul tells us that the resurrection occurs at the Second Coming. However, he also adds an additional event which follows some time after the Second Coming, namely, that Christ will hand over all rule and authority to God.

At the end of chapter 15 (verses 50 to 56), Paul returns to the events of the Resurrection. He introduces the subject by telling us that 'flesh and blood cannot inherit the Kingdom of God'. In other words, he declares that those who are expecting to receive the Kingdom will not do so in their mortal bodies because they are perishable and the perishable cannot inherit the imperishable. This means, by default, that some kind of transition will occur in those who will inherit the Kingdom. He goes on to say in verse 51, 'we shall not all sleep but we shall all be changed'. Thus, he confirms that not only those who are dead (sleeping) at the coming of the Kingdom will be translated into an imperishable form, but also those who are alive.

In verse 52, Paul tells us something of the speed and also of the timing of this event. He says it will be instantaneous ('in a moment, in the twinkling of an eye'), and that it will occur 'at the last trumpet'. In Isaiah 27:13 we see that 'in that day' (a reference to the coming of the Messiah) a great trumpet blast will be heard which will be the signal for Jews to come back and worship at Jerusalem. This may or may not be the 'last trumpet'. The same phrase, 'a great trumpet' is used in Matthew 24:31 to signal the gathering of the elect (see chapter 13 above). What is clear is that a 'last trumpet' will sound and that will be the signal for the dead in Christ to rise.

1 Thessalonians 4:13 -18 – Those who have died in Christ

Prior to this passage, in 1 Thessalonians 3:13, Paul has stated that the coming of the Lord will be with 'all his saints' indicating that Jesus will bring with him those who have believed in Him, both living and dead.

In 1 Thessalonians 4:13, Paul returns once more to the theme of those who have already died and in so doing opens up for us some other aspects concerning the coming of the Lord. He states clearly in verse 14 that Jesus (or to be precise, 'God') 'will bring with Him' those who have already died. He goes on to say once again that 'at the trumpet of God' the dead in Christ will rise first. Thus, it is confirmed that the Resurrection occurs at the last trumpet which is concurrent with the Second Coming ('the Lord himself will descend'). Once the dead have been raised and caught up with Him, those who are alive at that time will also be caught up with them 'to meet the Lord in the air', and from that moment on will be always with Him. From 1 Corinthians 15:52 (see above) we know that this is the point at which both the living and the dead who are His will receive imperishable bodies.

1 Thessalonians 5: 1- 11 - The 'Thief in the Night'

In chapter 5, Paul goes on to talk specifically about the 'day of the Lord', and its timing.

Several passages in the New Testament use the phrase 'thief in the night' to describe the Second Coming. This would suggest that there is something hidden or surreptitious about His coming, however, the context of this phrase in these passages is that for those not expecting the return of Christ, He will come like a thief in the night (see Matthew 24:42-43, 1 Thessalonians 5:1-11, and 2 Peter 3:10).

In all of these passages there are 2 elements:

1. We are to be on the alert (cf. Matthew 25:1-30 – Parable of the Virgins and the Talents), serving the master faithfully and watching for His coming. In this context we can observe the signs of the times (Matthew 24:32-33 – Parable of the fig Tree) and be ready at His coming and not drunk.
2. For those who do not know Him, the Lord's coming will be sudden and unexpected and judgement will come upon them 'suddenly like labour pains upon a woman with child and they will not escape' (1 Thessalonians 5:3).

There is no sense in any of these passages that Jesus' coming will be unexpected for us unless we are backslidden, living in disobedience and have allowed our oil to burn low. In fact, in 1 Thessalonians 5:4, Paul says, 'but you, brethren, are not in darkness, that the day would overtake you like a thief.'

2 Thessalonians 1

In 2 Thessalonians we have some of the clearest teaching on the End Times in all of the Pauline epistles. Clearly this was a subject that aroused some interest after Paul's first letter to the Thessalonians and so in his second letter he seeks to address some of their questions.

He begins by speaking of the suffering and persecution under which the Thessalonians were clearly afflicted. He refers them to the fact that this suffering will be relieved at the coming of the Lord (v.7). However, he goes on in verse 8 to state that the coming of the Lord will also be a time of retribution for those who do not 'obey the gospel of our Lord Jesus'. For the 'saints', this day will be a time when Jesus will 'be glorified' and 'marvelled at among all who have believed'.

2 Thessalonians 2

In the second chapter of 2 Thessalonians, Paul gives us a description of 'the Man of Lawlessness' (the Antichrist). In this passage, some facts are revealed:

- 'Apostasy' (falling away from the faith) will occur prior to the coming of the Antichrist (v.3).
- The Day of the Lord will not occur until after these events (v.3) i.e. after the Antichrist has been revealed.
- The Antichrist is also known as 'the son of destruction'.
- He will seat himself in the 'seat in the temple' exalting himself above all gods or objects of worship (v.4).
- He is restrained from being revealed now by some influence (v.6).
- At some time, the restraining influence will be taken out of the way and the Antichrist will be revealed (v.7).
- In the end, the Antichrist will be slain by the Lord at His coming (v.8).
- The revelation of the Antichrist will be,

* In accordance with the activity of Satan (v.9)
* With power and signs and false wonders (v.9)
* With wicked deception for those who do not receive the truth 'so as to be saved' (v.10)

- Those who have already chosen not to be saved will come under a deluding influence so that they will believe in the Antichrist (v.11) leading to judgement

2 Peter 3 & Jude

In the third chapter of Peter's second letter, the Apostle turns his attention to the return of Christ. He begins by saying that in the last days many will mock the Christian belief in the Second Coming because it has not yet occurred (v.3-5). Jude also confirms this in Jude 18. Peter affirms that as surely as God created the world out of water and destroyed it with water, so he is preserving it for a judgement of fire which will also be the time of the 'destruction of ungodly men' (v.6-7). He then encourages the reader to recognise that time has a different meaning to God compared with us ('one day is like a thousand years' (v.8)). The reason for the delay is that God is allowing grace to work to its maximum effect in giving people time to repent (v.9).

In verse 10, Peter restates the notion of the 'thief in the night' (see above) to depict the suddenness of the end. Clearly in this verse, Peter equates the Day of the Lord with the destruction of the earth. He goes on to add in verse 12 that the heavens will also be destroyed at this time. The consequence of the destruction of heaven and earth will be that eventually a new heavens and a new earth will be created (v.13) 'in which righteousness dwells'. Peter affirms that it is upon the new creation that his hope is set.

Summary

The teaching in the Epistles confirms and expands upon the teaching of Jesus. Much of this teaching focuses specifically upon the resurrection and its timing, although 2 Thessalonians 2 gives additional details concerning the Antichrist.

Essentially, we can say that:

- The day of the Lord will come suddenly for those not looking for it

- The righteous dead will be raised to life at the coming of the Lord and the righteous living will be caught up with them and transformed into their immortal states
- The rise of the Antichrist will be concluded at the coming of the Lord who will destroy him
- The earth will also be destroyed or at least devastated prior to the coming of the Lord (see chapter 11 concerning the judgements of the book of Revelation).

Section 4

Conclusion

Chapter 15

The Marriage Supper of the Lamb, the Judgements, Resurrection, Hell, and the New Heavens and Earth

Introduction

The purpose of this chapter is to tie up the loose ends and complete our study of the End Times. There are a number of items which occur during or after the end time period which we have mentioned or skipped over during this study. The intention here is to bring some explanation concerning these items.

The Marriage Supper of the Lamb

The timing of the Marriage Supper of the lamb has been a matter of some debate and is seen by some as being only for Christians who have been raptured prior to the Tribulation. Even a cursory look at Revelation 19:1-10 in context shows that this event only occurs following the destruction of Babylon the Great at the end of the Tribulation. It is upon her destruction, which is the vengeance of the saints whom she has persecuted, that the bride is finally ready (19:7).

Also, if we assume that there is a pre-Tribulation rapture, those saints who come to faith during the Tribulation are excluded from this event.

The passage which follows this (Revelation 19:11-19) deals directly with the coming of Christ to earth. Thus, within the context, the Marriage Supper of the Lamb is sandwiched between the destruction of Babylon and the Second Coming. From our previous studies, this point is synonymous with a post-Tribulation rapture. At this point, we have the snatching up of the Church - the bride who has made herself ready for the marriage to the bridegroom.

The Judgements

The end time judgements are recorded in the following passages: Revelation 19:21, Matthew 25:31-46, Joel 3:1-17, Zechariah 14:1-15.

A Biblical View of Judgement

Essentially, there are a number of facets to the notion of judgement in the Bible:

1. There is a continuing process of judgement ('God gave them over...' Romans 1:24, 26, 28) and a final Day of Judgement (Revelation 20:12).
2. Paul speaks of a judgement seat of Christ (2 Corinthians 5:10) and of the judgement seat of God (Romans 14:10). These terms are used inter-changeably.
3. Non-acceptance of God's provision in Christ merits condemnation (Revelation 20:13).
4. Any judgement made by God must inherently be just by reason of his righteous character.
5. Judgement is expressed via the wrath of God (Revelation 16:1).
6. Judgement includes believers and unbelievers (Romans 14:10).

2 Corinthians 5:10 says, 'We shall all stand before the judgement seat of Christ'.

Three Judgements

Essentially, if we study these passages, we see that there are actually three judgements:

1. The Judgement of the Nations at the Second Coming.

2. The Judgement of the Unrighteous.
3. The Judgement of the Righteous.

It can be argued that they occur as three distinct events during the End Times or that they occur simultaneously.

The Judgement of the Nations at the Second Coming

The judgement of the nations is dealt with above in Chapter 9 and Chapter 13. Suffice to say that God is storing up judgement for the nations of the world based on how they have treated the Jewish nation. The passage in Matthew 25:31-46 is not about the judgement of the unrighteous but specifically about the judgement of the nations, and it is nations who will be judged at Christ's return. At this point some of these nations will cease to exist; others will continue on into the Millennium.

Joel refers to this judgement in the chapter 3 verses 1-2 of his book:

> *For behold, in those days and at that time,*
> *When I restore the fortunes of Judah and Jerusalem,*
> *I will gather the nations*
> *And bring them down to the valley of Jehoshaphat.*
> *Then I will enter into judgement with them there*
> *On behalf of my people and My inheritance, Israel,*
> *Whom they have scattered among the nations;*
> *And they have divided up my land.*

The outcome will be that the 'goat' nations will be sent directly to hell, the place prepared for the Devil and his angels. The remaining nations will remain on earth and will live under Christ's authority through the Millennium.

The Judgement of the Unrighteous

According to Revelation 20:11-15, the second judgement occurs at the end of the Millennium (Revelation 20:5). At this point, the unbelieving dead are raised to life (or brought back from Sheol (Hebrew) or Hades

(Greek) – the place of waiting (see below)), and appear before the Great White Throne to be judged so that their eternal destiny can be determined. Those whose names are not in the book of life are cast into Hell where, Satan, the Antichrist and the False Prophet already reside.

This judgement will spell the end of all sin and rebellion against the authority and holiness of almighty God. Only those whose names are written in the Book of Life will pass through this judgement. But if the righteous have already been raised to life at the coming of Christ, who will fall into this category? Clearly it does not include those who have made a clear and definite commitment to Christ. We must speculate at this point and assume that God, the righteous judge, will show mercy upon those who have responded to the revelation they have received, however small and however distorted. This may include tribes whom the gospel has never reached. One thing we can be sure of, from the passage in revelation, some will receive God's mercy during this judgement and proceed to the new heaven and the new earth.

The Judgement of the Righteous

The unbelievers will be judged on the basis of the salvation of God. Believers will be judged for their works and here is introduced the notion of rewards. The exact timing of this event is not clear from scripture. It may occur at the final judgement alongside the judgement of the unrighteous or, as some argue, it may occur prior to the Millennium so that those who reign with Christ during the Millennium will already have been judged and have received their rewards. The following summarises what is clear from scripture:

1. God will give rewards on the basis of what has been done in this life (Matthew 6:1).
2. The rewards are partially received here but mostly reserved for heaven (Matthew 10:40-42, Luke 16:9, Matthew 25:14-30).
3. The final rewards will be reserved for the Day of Judgement (Matthew 25:14-30).
4. The rewards are of a spiritual nature like 'the crown of righteousness', but their character is not otherwise specified (2 Timothy 4:8).
5. There is no suggestion that salvation itself comes under the category of a reward (Ephesians 2:1-10).

In the parable of the talents (Matthew 24:14-30), there is certainly the notion of responsibility in the new Kingdom being a reward for righteous service. There is also the notion of punishment for those who do not serve their master well.

Resurrection

The Resurrection has already been discussed in Chapter 14 when considering 1 Corinthians 15 and 1 Thessalonians 4. However, for further clarity we will consider the various theories concerning the post-death state of believers and unbelievers below prior to their resurrection. Specific passages concerning the Resurrection in the New Testament include: Revelation 20:1-10, John 5:25-32, 1 Corinthians 15, 1 Thessalonians 4:13-18. The following summarises the various views of the Resurrection.

What Happens When We Die

Three theories have been propounded by various scholars as to what happens to us when we die. They are summarised below.

Theory 1: Soul Sleep

This is the theory that after we die, we enter into some kind of comatose state from which we will be awoken at the return of the Lord. There are four scriptures which bring this theory into question:

1. Philippians 1:23 "But I am hard pressed from both directions, having the desire to depart and be with Christ". Here Paul does not envisage sleeping but being awake with the Lord.
2. 2 Corinthians 5:8 "We are of good courage, I say, and prefer rather to be absent from the body and to be at home with the Lord". Here again, Paul anticipates being in the presence of the Lord.
3. Luke 23:43 "...Truly I say to you, today you shall be with me in paradise". Whilst this does not preclude the thief on the cross being asleep whilst in Paradise, the inference is that he will knowledgeably be with the Lord.
4. Luke 16:22, the story of the Rich Man and Lazarus. This parable which Jesus told, if taken at face value, clearly demonstrates not

just consciousness for those who have departed this life but also the ability to be able to watch the events on earth unfolding.

Theory 2 Timelessness

This is the theory that when we die we immediately step outside of time and are transported instantaneously to the resurrection of the saints at the Second Coming. The same scriptures mentioned above tend to undermine this theory.

Theory 3 Bodily Resurrection at the Parousia

The theory that is most strongly supported from scripture begins with the fact that after His death, Jesus went into Hades. This is mentioned in 1 Peter 3:18-20. There He preached to those who had been judged in the flood. He took the keys of Death and Hades from the hands of Satan (Revelation 1:18). He rose from the dead and led forth a host of captives (Ephesians 4:7-10). He ascended on high (Psalm 24). The dead in Christ are now in paradise having ascended with him.

When Jesus returns, the dead in Christ (those who sleep, according to 1 Corinthians 15 – who are now in Paradise) will rise (i.e. come back into the time-space, temporal world we inhabit) and receive resurrection bodies which are imperishable – 1 Thessalonians 4:16 'The dead in Christ shall rise first'.

Those who remain at His coming will be caught up (harpazo – literally snatched up, seized with force contrasting with 'to steal secretly' (klepto) as a thief in 5:2) with them, and will receive resurrection bodies: "we shall not all sleep but we shall all be changed" (1 Corinthians 15:51).

Hell

Heaven and hell are both an eternal reality, and one which we will all encounter sooner or later.

The Mediaeval notion of hell was that it is the place where Satan dwells. This was because of misunderstanding and mistranslation which mixed up Hell with Hades. The former is the place of eternal punishment and the latter is the place of residence for departed souls.

The image of Satan surrounded by demons and fire is currently incorrect; however, it will one day be accurate, after he is finally judged (Revelation 20:10). Satan resides at present in the second heaven.

1. The Meaning of 'Hell'

There are two words used in the New Testament which have been translated as 'Hell': Hades and Gehenna.

Hades (Sheol – in the Old Testament) refers to the place where departed spirits of the unredeemed go to await judgement and is usually associated directly with death: 'death and hell'.

Gehenna, on the other hand, is derived from the name for the Valley of Hinnom, which is a deep, narrow glen to the south of Jerusalem. In 2 Kings 23:10, Jeremiah 7:3 and 19:2-6, it speaks of the practice of the Israelites, prior to the captivity, of offering up their children in sacrifice to the God Moloch, by burning them in the fire. This took place in the Valley of Hinnom.

By the New Testament times, the valley was Jerusalem's refuse tip. Fires would be burning continually in the valley to burn up the rubbish deposited there. The Dung Gate opened up over it so that people could throw their waste into it. All in all it was a smelly, dangerous, horrible place for utterly destroying all used or unwanted items. Jesus uses this image to capture what Hell will be like.

2. Jesus Refers to Hell

Within the gospels, Jesus makes a number of references to Hell as a place of judgement as follows:

a. Matthew 5:22, "...and whoever shall say, 'you fool'. Shall be guilty enough to go into the fiery hell."
b. Matthew 5:29-30, Matthew 18:8-9, "...and if your right hand makes you stumble..."
c. Matthew 10:28, "And do not fear those who kill the body but are unable to kill the soul, but rather fear Him who is able to destroy both soul and body in hell."
d. Matthew 23:15, 33, "...twice as much a son of hell..." Righteousness through the Law without the Spirit leads to hell.

3. Who Goes to Hell?

It is not for us to say who specifically will end up in Hell. Judgement is God's prerogative. That is why we should not judge each other because in so doing, we put ourselves in the place of God. One thing is for sure, there are going to be some surprises both in Hell and in Heaven.

Nobody will go to Hell (Gehenna) for their sins. They will go to Hell for rejecting the solution to their sins. Jesus has done everything that was required for nobody to go to Hell. He took the punishment that was ours. He has been to Hell (Hades) on our behalf so that we do not have to go either to Hades or to Gehenna. It is up to us to take this message to the world.

It is not that God will send people to Hell but that they are already going there unless they can be rescued. It is as if they are sitting on a train with Hell as their destination. Every now and again, the train stops to allow them to get off, but they stay on because they are more comfortable, all their friends and relatives are still on board, they are afraid to step off, they just can't believe there is any other train to ride on, or that they don't actually believe the train exists. The task of Christians is to stand on the platform and warn them of the disaster at the end of the track as well as to tell them of the wonderful (though sometimes hard) walk to paradise that we are on.

Those who will definitely be in Hell include: Satan, the Beast and the False Prophet (Revelation 20:10-15), and all of Satan's cohorts (2 Peter 2:4).

4. What Will Hell Be Like

Hell (Gehenna) is constantly referred to as being 'a lake of fire' which never goes out (Revelation 19:20, 20:10, 14, 15). It is also referred to as the 'second death'. Furthermore it is described as a place of torment. Some say that this language is figurative and symbolic. What we do know is that it is a place of judgement and that it is away from the presence of God (2 Thessalonians 1:9).

Hopefully, no one reading this book will ever have to find out.

The New Heaven and the New Earth

There is much we could say about heaven from scripture but that should be the subject of a separate book in its own right. The following provides a very brief summary:

The third Heaven is the presence of God himself.

a. Jesus has gone to prepare a place there (John 14:1-4).
b. Both Paul (2 Corinthians 12:2) and John (Rev 4:1) were taken there in spirit.
c. Locationally, we do not know where it is. Scripture is not clear except to say that where it is, the presence of God is also.

At the end of Revelation (Revelation 21:1- 22:3) we see the creation of a new heaven and a new earth. We do not know if these comprise the place that Jesus went to prepare or if He is going to start again from scratch. What we do know is that our future will be glorious, residing with God Himself and with his Son in his new and perfect creation!

Chapter 16

An End Times Scenario

Introduction

We have largely concluded our perilous journey through the scriptures identifying and interpreting those which relate specifically to the End Times. All that remains is to try and put these events into some kind of order to enable the reader to visualise the scene at the close of the age.

I do not, for a moment, assume that the following scenario will be played out to the letter. As I stated in the introduction, there is only one version of the End Times which will come to pass and that is God's. Also, I do not mind if the reader wishes to disagree with my interpretation. My purpose has been to look at the appropriate scriptures and give an interpretation which will at least inform the reader and at best assist them in thinking through some of these themes in order to draw their own conclusions.

Having said all of that, please bear with me whilst I seek to paint the End Times scene.

Lights! Camera! Action!

Currently, we live in a time during which the world is re-aligning itself. After the first Gulf War, George Bush began talking in terms of a New World Order, and since then (and especially since 9/11) we have seen USA beginning to position itself as the police force of the world with the self-appointed role of dealing with any who would threaten world peace (or at least threaten the security of the USA).

The point of confrontation is currently with the Muslim world. However this plays out, we will come to a time where the world is aligned into ten self-governing regions, all based around the system of monarchical democracy. The gathering of the nation of Israel back to the land will continue throughout this period.

A time of unrest will arise when some of these regions will go to war and one of the leaders of these nations will conquer three of the other regions to bring stability. It is on the back of this that he will become elected as the One World Leader, in command of all of the ten regions. It is also at this time that he will make a covenant with Israel presumably to protect it against its aggressive neighbours. This will signal the commencement of the time known as The Great Tribulation.

At this point, due to the international unrest, death through war, famine and disease will be unleashed on the world. Natural disasters will follow, including meteorite showers and other natural phenomena. All of these will be part of God's judgement upon the earth.

In the middle of this seven year period the world leader will break the covenant he has made with Israel and will come up against Jerusalem in war. At some time during this battle, he will appear to be killed but will 'arise from the dead' to the astonishment of the whole world. God will cause many of the nation of Israel to flee to Jordan for protection and, at this point, this leader will turn his attentions towards the persecution of the Church.

He will also implement a new system of monetary exchange, probably as a result of the hyper-inflation caused by the international crisis, whereby each citizen will be given a number to use in order to trade. Those who do not accept this number will not be able to trade except through the black market. The Minister of Propaganda will assist the world leader in persuading the citizens of the world to adopt this system and through it they will see this leader as their saviour. The outcome of this will be that he will be honoured by means of a statue on the altar in the temple in Jerusalem (which will have been rebuilt by this time).

The natural disasters will continue and God will raise up two men who will speak against the world leader and his government for a period of 3 ½ years. At first, this opposition will be seen as nothing more than an irritation, but eventually, the leader will have these men publicly and summarily killed.

At this point, the world leader will lead the international armies once more against Jerusalem and they will capture the city and kill many Jews present there at the time. He will also send his armies against those hiding in Jordan, and, just when he has the remaining Jews surrounded and is about to move in for the kill, Christ will return and rescue his people. He will bring with him the ancient saints and the Church, who will have just been raptured, and as he arrives on the scene, landing upon the Mount of Olives, all remaining Jews will recognise him as the Messiah who was 'pierced' at their hands. They will throw themselves on his mercy and acknowledge him as their Lord.

He will begin his judgement on the nations, starting with the world leader and his minister of propaganda, who will be despatched from the earth. He will then deal with the armies of all nations gathered against his people in Jordan and in Jerusalem.

Having completed this judgement, he will set up in Jerusalem the seat of his government over the world and all remaining nations will submit to his reign. Once the clear up operation of the world, and especially of the land of Israel, has been completed The Lord will reign justly over all nations. Since the world economic system (Babylon) will have collapsed, he will establish trade on the basis of godly principles and righteousness. Those who submit to his rule will be blessed; those who do not, will not be blessed. He will receive tribute from them annually and will cause God's blessing to be withheld from those who do not bring tribute to him. Those who have returned with him will assist him in exercising his governmental and administrative rule over all the earth.

His reign on earth will last for a significant period of time, at the end of which he will allow Satan some freedom once more to test the loyalty of the nations. Some will be deceived and will ally with Satan to come up against him once more. But he will deal with them once and for all, and will confine Satan to hell for eternity.

At this point, the final judgement will be held. Those who have previously died, and whose souls are in Hades, will be released in order to stand trial before God's throne. Those whose names are not written in the book of life will at this point be dispatched to hell. The righteous will also be judged and will be rewarded according to their righteous deeds as Saints whilst upon the earth.

Following the judgement, the old heaven and earth will pass away and a new heaven and earth will be created. They will exist in perfect harmony under the rulership of Christ who will illumine the world for his people, the New Jerusalem.

Hallelujah, for the Lord our God, the Almighty, reigns.

Let us rejoice and be glad and give the glory to him.

Appendix 1. The Babylonian Kings

Nebuchadnezzar
Reigned 605 – 562 BC

Evil-merodach (Amul Marduk) – 562-560
Son of Nebuchadnezzar. Reigned 2 yrs, was dissolute and was murdered by his brother-in-law, Neriglissar, who seized the throne. (2 Kings 25:27-30, Jeremiah 52:31-34).

Neriglissar (Nergal Sharusar) 560-556
Jeremiah 39:3-13. Son-in-law of Neuchadnezzar.

Labashi Marduk (Laborosoachad) May & June 556
Son of Neriglissar. He met with a violent end after 2 months at the hand of conspirators led by Nabonidus.

Nabonidus & Belshazzar 556 - 539
Nabonidus married a daughter of Nebuchadnezzar, Nitocris. She is the Queen who later reminds Belshazzar, her son, about Daniel when he has seen the writing on the wall.
Belshazzar reigned as co-regent from 553 BC, and was the ruler of the province of Babylon. His father stayed with his army on manoeuvres in the desert for the last ten years of his life.

Cyrus & Darius (559 – 530 B.C. (539 overthrew Babylon)).
Cyrus was king of the Medo-Persian Empire and came against Babylon around 542 BC. A number of battles occurred before he conquered the Babylonian army, led by Nobonidus, and overthrew Babylon itself, ruled by Belshazzar.
Cyrus entered the palace and slew the king and his lords, and took possession of the city. "In that night", says the sacred record, "was Belshazzar, the king of the Chaldeans slain."

Appendix 2. The Successors of Alexander the Great

Alexander expanded the Greek Empire between 331-321 BC. He was born in 356 BC; was educated under Aristotle; and became king of Macedonia in 335 BC. He ruled as far west as Egypt and as far east as India. He ruled as an absolute monarch until 321 BC.

In verse 4 of Daniel 11 we see the four divisions of his empire, subsequent to his death. The words 'not through his own descendents' refer to the fact that although Alexander left two sons, neither of them became king: both were murdered.

Following the death of Alexander, none of his successors extended the Kingdom to the extent that Alexander had.

i. Lysimachus took Thrace and Bythinia
ii. Cassander took Macedonia and Greece
iii. Ptolemy took Egypt, Palestine and Edom - line of Cleopatra
iv. Seleucus took Syria, Babylonia and the East to the Indus river.

From verse 5 onwards of Daniel 11, the vision of Daniel is only concerned with the king of Syria and the king of Egypt because it is only these two who affect 'the Beautiful Land'.

The southern line, the line of the king of Egypt was as follows:

- Ptolemy 1st Soter 323 – 285 BC (11:5)
- Ptolemy 2nd Philadelphus 284-246 BC (11.6)
- Ptolemy 3rd Euergetes 246-221 BC (11:7-9)
- Ptolemy 4th Philopater 221-204 BC (11:10-12)
- Ptolemy 5th Epiphanes 204-181 BC (11: 14-17)
- Ptolemy 6th Philometor 181-145 BC (11: 25-27)

The Northern line, the line of the king of Syria was as follows:

- Seleucus 1st Nacator 312-280 BC (11:5)
- Antiochus 1st Soter 280-261BC (not mentioned in the Daniel account)

- Antiochus 2nd Theos 261-246 BC (11: 6)
- Seleucus 2nd Callinicus 246-226 BC (11:7-9)
- Seleucus 3rd Ceraunus 226-223 BC (11:10)
- Antiochus 3rd (the Great) 223-187 BC (11:10-19)
- Seleucus 4th Philopater 187-175 BC (11: 20)
- Antiochus 4th Epiphanes 175-164 BC (11: 21-35)
- Antiochus 5th Eupator 164-162 BC
- Antiochus 1st Soter 162-150 BC
- Alexander Balas (150-145 BC

The last 3 are not mentioned by Daniel.

Essentially, these verses, Daniel 11:5-20, give us the history of Syria and Egypt even though they were written in around 535BC, over 200 years before the events spoken of took place.

Verse 5 refers to Ptolemy 1st Soter. He took on the title of king after both of Alexander's sons had been killed in 306 BC. The Prince who 'gained ascendancy over him' is Seleucus 1st Nacator. Seleucus became one of Ptolemy's generals in 312 BC, and later became a king himself over Syria, Turkey, Babylonia, Media etc. and therefore he did become more powerful than Ptolemy.

Between verse 5 and verse 6, 60 years elapse. The actions described in verse 6 take place in 252 BC.

The king of the South is Ptolemy 2nd Philadelphus and his daughter is Berenice. The king of the North is Antiochus 2nd Ferros. The two had been fighting and therefore, Ptolemy wanted to gain dominion over Syria. By this action, (the alliance and the marriage of the king of the south to the king of the north) Antiochus 2nd was forced by Ptolemy (who was stronger) to divorce his wife Laodice and to marry Berenice. As a result of this, the two sons of Laodice were disinherited because the agreement was that the 1st son of Berenice would become the successor of Antiochus. Three years after the marriage, Ptolemy died and Berenice was divorced by Antiochus and the plans were thwarted. Antiochus then retook Laodice as his wife. Laodice by this time was wary of her husband's fickleness and so after the wedding ceremony she has had her husband poisoned and had her son, Seleucus 2nd Colunicus, proclaimed king of Syria. 'She will be given up' (v.6) is a reference to the fact that Laodice had Berenice, her son and her attendants murdered. Thus, Antiochus, Ptolemy and Berenice all were brought down as prophesied.

Verses 7 to 9 refer to the battles between Ptolemy 3rd Euergetes and Seleucus 2nd Colunicus, a war of revenge

Verse 7 says, 'One of the descendents of her line will arise', This is a reference to Berenice's brother, Ptolemy 3rd. Syria was invaded by Ptolemy 3rd to try and save Berenice who had taken refuge at the sanctuary of Daphne but he arrived too late and she had already been murdered. The reference in verse 7 to the 'fortress of the king' foreshadows the fact that he overthrew all of the Syrian fortresses all the way to the Tigris. He captured Laodice and had her executed.

Verse 8 is a description of the spoils of war taken back by him to Egypt (having their gods taken from them is extreme humiliation on a nation). He captured 2,500 statues, etc including Egyptian images which had been taken to Babylon by Cambyses, son of Cyrus, 200 years earlier. He also took loads of gold and silver. His name 'Euergetes' means benefactor which was given him because of the booty he brought back from Syria. 'He will refrain from attacking…' (verse 8): Ptolemy 3rd did not again attack Syria. In verse 9, the Syrian king, Seleucus 2nd attacks Egypt to gain vengeance. This happened around 240 BC but he was defeated and had to return to Syria empty-handed.

Verses 10 to 12 deal with Seleucus 3rd Ceraunus, Antiochus 3rd (the Great), and Ptolemy 4th Philopater

'His sons' (verse 10) is a reference to the sons of the Syrian King i.e. Seleucus 3rd, who died young in battle in Asia Minor, and Antiochus 3rd who succeeded his brother who became king at 18 years of age. 'He shall assemble a multitude of great forces' (v.10) – Antiochus 3rd assembled a huge force to attack Egypt. He waged several campaigns and restored Syrian authority as far south as Gaza.

After this he made two further campaigns. The first in 219 ended in stalemate but in the 2nd campaign (217 BC) he made battle at Raphia at the edge of the Sinai Peninsula. Thus, he had taken Phoenicia and Palestine and was on the border with Egypt. Raphia was in Egypt. Philopater was lazy and wasn't worried about losing the territory to Syria until Antiochus entered Egypt and 'was enraged' (v.11). He went forth to fight, taking his sister Arsimae who was also his wife. Ptolemy assembled an army of 70,000 soldiers, 5,000 cavalry and 73 battle elephants. The multitude of Syria (62,000 soldiers, cavalry of 6,000 and 102 elephants) was given into the hands of the Egyptian king.

In verse 12, we see that the heart of Ptolemy 3rd was 'lifted up' with pride. He killed 10,000 of the Syrian infantry, 300 cavalry, and 5 elephants and took 40,000 prisoners, leaving the Syrians with a token army. In addition, Antiochus was nearly captured as he fled in defeat. 'He will not prevail' (v.12) - Ptolemy could have gone on to absolutely defeated Syria but was too lazy to do so. Ptolemy and his wife both died soon thereafter, assassinated by their own people.

Verses 13 to 19 continue with Antiochus 3rd but also deal with Ptolemy 5th Epiphanes.

In Verse 13 we see Antiochus 3rd's third campaign against Egypt (201BC) which he waged having spent the previous 12 years gathering strength by conquering as far east as India and as far north as the Caspian Sea.

In verse 14 we are told that there are conspirators in the Southern Kingdom against Ptolemy 5th who was an infant (4 years old) when he assumed the throne. Philip 5th of Macedon also agreed with Antiochus to go against Egypt to divide the spoils and attacked Egyptian possessions in the Aegean Sea. 'The violent ones among your people…' (v.14) - Antiochus 3rd was helped by Jews who led a rebellion against Ptolemy under Tobias who attacked the Egyptian garrison in Jerusalem and took it over so that they could establish divisions amongst the foreign rulers in order to free Israel from domination. However, they merely fell under the dominion of the Syrians.

In verse 16, we see that Antiochus 3rd defeated Egypt (201 BC). By 191 BC, Palestine was under full control of the Syrians. Verse 15 refers to the fact that Antiochus 3rd besieged Sidon in Phoenicia (Lebanon). In 198 BC the Syrians were driven back out of Palestine by an Egyptian general named Scopus. He came against Syria but was defeated at Paneas (which became known as Caesarea Philippi) in 198 BC. Scopus fled to Sidon and therefore Antiochus besieged Sidon until Sidon surrendered. The Egyptians sent three forces to try and rescue Scopus but failed. In verse 16 we see that Antiochus 3rd was able to impose his will on Egypt. Antiochus then had control of Israel. The word 'destruction' should be translated 'completion' He did not enter Israel to destroy it but to confirm his conquest. For the first three years of his conquest, the people of Israel did not have to pay taxes; for the next three years they only had to pay two thirds of their taxes. He also freed the temple priests, Levites, etc. from the necessity to pay taxes.

As a result of the fact that Antiochus was being threatened by Rome he came to Egypt to make peace (verse 17), offering his daughter, Cleopatra (not the famous one) to Ptolemy 5th Epiphanes in the year 197 BC. Ptolemy was only 7 at the time so the marriage was only consummated 5 years later when Ptolemy was 12. By offering his daughter, Antiochus hoped to corrupt the kingship of Egypt because he expected his daughter to side with her father; however, she sided with her husband against her father. He took his campaigns into Asia Minor (verse 18), aided by Hannibal, to come against the rising power of Rome who were assisting Egypt. He took Thrace and parts of Greece in 196 BC. The 'Commander' in verse 18 was the Roman Consul Lucius Cornelius Scipio Asiaticus who was the brother of Scipio Africanus who had defeated Hannibal and destroyed Carthage. In 191 BC he defeated Antiochus at Thermopylae. In 191 BC he defeated Antiochus at Maendar, on the Magnesae River, south-west of Ephesus. He told the Romans they had no business in Asia but in 181 BC he was forced to accept the peace of Aramea and had to abondon Asia Minor to Rome.

Verse 19 refers to the death of Antiochus 3rd. He returned in defeat and had to give tribute to Rome. He started to plunder temples in order to be able to pay the tribute. Whilst doing so in Elam, he was killed, in the year 187 BC.

Seleucus 4th Philopater sent 'an oppressor' (verse 20), Heliodorus, to collect taxes from all lands, especially from the Jews to be extracted from the temple treasury. He ruled for 11 years and was poisoned by Heliodorus.

In verse 21, Antiochus Epiphanes is described as 'despicable'. He was not the rightful heir but an illegitimate son of Antiochus 3rd. He pretended to be the guardian of the son of Antiochus 3rd but developed a plot and had young Antiochus murdered by Andronicus and then had Andronicus murdered. Hence it describes him as one 'on whom the honour of kingship has not been conferred' and that he will 'seize the Kingdom by intrigue'.

In verse 22, we see again the imagery of a flood being used to describe an army. In this context, he defeated the troops of Heliodotus and then the troops of Egypt which were trying to retake Palestine. 'The Prince of the Covenant' described here is the High Priest, Onius, who was murdered by Antiochus with the help of Onius' brother, Menelaus, in 172 BC.

Verse 23 describes his actions in making allegiances with Egypt and others. His sister, Cleopatra was married to Ptolemy previously, and was the current Queen Mother. He went up with only a small force, because of his father's previous defeat by Rome, against Egypt.

Verse 24 tells us 'he will enter the richest parts of the realm'. He went after the most fertile provinces in order to use the plunder to gain favours 'for a time' which was 12 years.

In verses 25 -26 his first Egyptian campaign against Ptolemy 6th Philometor, one of the 2 sons of Cleopatra, one of his nephews, is described. He went against Egypt for the control of Palestine because it had been given to Cleopatra as a dowry by Antiochus 3rd. The first battle took place in 170 BC. The battle was fought in North Sinai at Mount Cassius and at Pelusium. Ptolemy lost and was captured by Antiochus, due to treachery in his own ranks.

Verse 27 describes the fact that after Ptolemy was captured, the people of Alexandria made his brother king, Ptolemy 7th Euergetes. Antiochus pretended to Philometor that he was going to attack Egypt to put him back on the throne; Philometor pretended to believe him 'they will speak lies to each other at the same table' (v.27). Their plan failed since Antiochus only succeeded in making Philometor king of Memphis but was repelled at Alexandria. The two brothers established a joint rule and Philometor married his sister, Cleopatra (named after his / her mother).

In verse 28 Antiochus returned to his own land with much plunder but without having conquered Egypt. His heart was set against Israel, 'the Holy Covenant'. Jason, brother of Menelaus, had rebelled against Menelaus, now High Priest in Israel and on his way through, Antiochus put down the rebellion of Jason.

Verses 29 to 30 describe Antiochus third campaign against Egypt in 168 BC, which took place after he had found out about the agreement of the 2 brothers (Philometor and Euergetes). 'Kittim' in this verse is a reference to Cyprus. Roman galleys came into Egypt which had previously been anchored at Cyprus. Antiochus was met at Alexandria by a force under a Roman general named Gaius Popillius Laenas who ordered Antiochus to leave Egypt. The Roman general drew a circle around Antiochus with a sword and told him to make his decision before he left the circle. Antiochus was thus publicly humiliated and forced to withdraw.

Verses 30 to 35 describe his persecution of the Jews. He 'shows regard' for the apostate, Hellenising Jews who followed Menelaeus, 'those who forsake the holy covenant' (v.30).

In verse 31 we see the abomination of desolation. A pig was offered on the altar in the temple and the daily sacrifice was done away with. They also erected an image of Zeus Olympus in the temple and offered sacrifices of swine to it. Observance of the Sabbath and of circumcision was forbidden and Greek soldiers had orgies in the temple precincts.

Verse 32 describes how he elevated the apostates. However, the Maccabees revolted and defeated every army sent against them by Antiochus. Hasadim, the righteous ones in Israel, 'those who have insight' (v.33) maintained the law by setting up underground teaching schools to make known the law. But many were tortured and killed. In verse 34 we see described the putting down of the rebellion, as all of the Maccabee brothers were killed.

Appendix 3 Gog and Magog

In studies of the End Times, the question of the identities of Gog and Magog are often postulated. The following article details the historic identities of these peoples. Whilst the author does not agree in full with the content of this article, particularly around the suggestion of an end time spiritual revival, the article is included here in its entirety for completeness.

Is the Soviet Union Gog and Magog?

By Jay Rogers

http://www.forerunner.com/forerunner/X0664_Gog_and_Magog.htm

Is the Soviet Union mentioned in the Bible?

Many people, searching to discover the answer to this question, have studied Ezekiel chapters 38 and 39 in an attempt to find the role of this (former) communist superpower in the End Times:

> *And the word of the Lord came to me saying: 'Son of man, set your face toward Gog of the land of Magog, the prince of Rosh, Meshech, and Tubal, and prophesy against Him, and say, "Thus says the Lord God, 'Behold I am against you, O Gog, prince of Rosh, Meshech, and Tubal. And I will turn you about, and put hooks in your jaws, and I will bring you out, and all your army, horses and horsemen, all of them splendidly attired, a great company with buckler and shield, all of them wielding swords; Persia, Ethiopia, and Put with them, all of them with shield and helmet; Gomer with all its troops; Beth-togarmah from the remote parts of the north with all its troops - many peoples with you (Ezekiel 38:1-6).*

Many have interpreted the vivid apocalyptic imagery in Ezekiel 38 and 39 as foretelling a war between the Soviet Union and the restored nation of Israel just before the Second Coming of Jesus. Others have understood this vision as a prophecy which was fulfilled in the 2nd century B.C. at the defeat of the Assyrian invaders of Palestine by Judas Maccabeus.

In order to gain an understanding of these chapters, it is useful to employ a method of interpretation which rightly discerns the nature of apocalyptic literature. Apocalyptic passages in the Bible serve a dual purpose: to comfort God's people in times of tribulation, and to show them that they are only a small part of a universal struggle between the forces of good and evil in which the Kingdom of God will ultimately emerge as victorious. Apocalyptic messages are designed to increase the faith of God's people in times of national crisis by assuring them that their God is able to deliver them.

Ezekiel 38-39 should be understood in the context of its apocalyptic literary style; this is a highly visionary passage depicting an earthly struggle of Ezekiel's time which is only a smaller reflection of a spiritual conflict between the forces of heaven and hell.

Historically, the nations mentioned in this passage, Magog, Meshech, Tubal, Gomer and Beth-togarmah, were a barbarous people known as the Scythians. These were a nomadic people who had moved from central Asia to southern Russia. Just about the same time that Ezekiel was born, the Scythians terrorized southwest Asia and the Middle East.

Horsemen Splendidly Attired

Pouring through the passes of the Caucasus mountains, hordes of Scythians covered the fertile plains of the south. Known and feared for their ruthless cruelty, they came like a flight of locusts, devouring the countryside, consuming crops, slaughtering livestock, burning homes and villages, and massacring the inhabitants of the land.

The Scythians were fierce tribesmen who were paid no wage unless they could produce scalps of enemy soldiers killed in battle. Every Scyth owned at least one horse used for riding into battle. All carried a double curved bow, shooting over the horse's left shoulder. Arrows and bow were carried in a case slung from the left side of a belt. The Scyths also carried swords, knives and daggers and wore bronze helmets and chain mail jerkins lined with red felt. They carried round shields decorated with central gold emblems in the shape of an animal.

The Scythians were accomplished horsemen, being among the first people to master the art of riding. This made their approach seem unnaturally sudden and gave them the great advantage of surprise attack. The Scythians advanced quickly south-westward striking fear into the hearts of the people of every nation that lay in their path.

One force appeared on Iran's border in the 8th century B.C. bringing them into fierce conflict with the Cimmerians. The Scythian horsemen drove the Cimmerian foot soldiers northward through the Caucasus Mountains across the Volga river. Another force chased the remnant of the Cimmerian army across Armenia, while a third force joined the second contingent at Lake Urmia and drove the remaining Cimmerian armies all the way across central Turkey into the regions of Phrygia and Lydia.

During the time of Ezekiel and Jeremiah, the Scythians attacked Syria and Judea from their capital city of Saqqez. Later, they attacked Egypt which borders Ethiopia and Libya (Put).

In the same year that the prophet Jeremiah was called (626 B.C.), swarms of Scythian invaders struck terror into the nations surrounding the Assyrian empire. Having made a pact with the Assyrians, Scythian horsemen were sent against Egypt and Judah.

Jeremiah, a contemporary of Ezekiel, foresaw an approaching storm, and described the coming invasion of the Babylonian empire. The early chapters of Jeremiah refer to the Scythian invasion which shortly preceded that of the Babylonians:

> *I am bringing evil from the north, and great destruction. A lion has gone up from his thicket, And a destroyer of nations has set out; He has gone out from his place To make your land a waste. Your cities will be ruins without inhabitant. Behold, he goes up like clouds, And his chariots are like the whirlwind; His horses are swifter than eagles. Woe to us, for we are ruined! (Jeremiah 4:6,7,13)*

The inclusion of the nations of Meshech, Tubal, Gomer, Beth-togarmah, Persia, Ethiopia and Put in Ezekiel 38:3,5,6 is best understood in the light of the historical context of the Scythian invasion.

- In Genesis 10:2, Magog, Meshech, Tubal, and Gomer are named as the sons of Japeth and are the founders of the northern group of nations from which the Scythians descended.
- In Ezekiel 27:13, Meshech and Tubal are mentioned as being sellers of slaves to Tyre; and in Ezekiel 32:26, they are spoken of as "instilling terror in the land of the living."
- Meshech is thought to be a people called the Moschi dwelling in the Caucasus mountain regions according to Assyrian inscriptions.

- Tubal is thought to be a people called the Tibareni dwelling on the southeast shores of the Black Sea.
- Gomer is thought to have been the Cimmerians, who occupied central Turkey in the days of the Assyrian empire.
- Beth-togarmah is thought to be Armenia.
- Persia is the people inhabiting the region of modern day Iraq and Iran.
- Ethiopia and Put speak of the Black African nations.

When the history of the Scythian people is examined, it becomes apparent that they are the people described in Ezekiel's prophecy. Herodotus, the Greek historian, refers to the suddenness of the Scythians attack on the Assyrian empire.

By examining this passage in its historical and cultural context, it can be seen that Ezekiel 38-39 describes the Scythian invasions during the time of Ezekiel. This passage also apocalyptically foresees the ultimate triumph of Jesus Christ and His victorious Kingdom over the Kingdoms of this world.

Telescoping

A characteristic of apocalyptic literature is telescoping or the compression of immediate historical judgments and which prefigure the ultimate judgment of God. An example of telescoping is found in Joel 1:4. The prophet Joel stated that a locust plague causing a famine in his day was "the day of the Lord" (Joel 1:15). Joel saw in the locust plague a prefiguring of final judgment. The two events are superimposed giving the hearer a sense of immanency.

The same phenomenon occurs in Ezekiel 38-39. The invasion of Judea by the Scythian armies is coupled with a vision of an almighty God ultimately vanquishing these forces:

> *'I shall strike your bow from your left hand, and dash down your arrows from your right hand. You shall fall on the mountains of Israel, you and all your troops, and the peoples who are with you; I shall give you as food to every kind of predatory bird and beast of the field. You will fall on the open field; for it is I who have spoken,' declares the Lord (Ezekiel 39:3-5).*

"Gog and Magog" is a biblical symbol for the heathen nations of the world. The Apostle John equates "the nations of the four corners of the earth" with "Gog and Magog" (Revelation 20:8). Thus, "Gog and Magog" is used in the Bible to denote the nations of the world that are opposed to Christ and His Kingdom.

The Bible tells us the Kingdom of God is destined to overcome all the nations of the world. One day these nations are going to stream into the Kingdom of God. In Psalm 2, we are told of a great King, ruling over a vast Kingdom that far transcends the boundaries of the nation Israel. This Psalm speaks of the heathen nations being given to Jesus Christ as His inheritance.

This great end time revival is likened to the invasion of the Scythian horsemen in Ezekiel 38-39. The suddenness of the Scythian's attack is superimposed on the vision of Jesus Christ moving quickly throughout the nations bringing spiritual awakening to the entire world prior to His return.

By interpreting Ezekiel 38-39 as an apocalyptic passage, it can be seen that this is not meant to be a prediction that the Soviet Union will one day invade a restored Israel. This is not to say that the Soviet Union won't invade Israel someday, but this is not what this passage is intended to mean.

Currently, the nations mentioned in Ezekiel's message are under the domination of Soviet influence. Nations such as Kazakh, Kirghiz, Tajik, Uzbek, Turkmen, Azerbaijan, Armenia, Georgia, Moldavia and the Ukraine are a part of the Soviet Union. These nations were overrun in ancient times by the Scythian hordes. Today there is great social upheaval occurring in these nations. Demonstrations calling for independence occur daily in these nations.

There is good reason to hope that a great awakening of God's Spirit will begin in a short time in these countries. The progress of this awakening will overthrow the yoke of atheistic communism and many of the people in these nations will begin to stream into the Kingdom of God.

Although God may choose to use a particular nation in some strategic way at a given point in history, His Kingdom and power to save are not bound by the governments and institutions of men. God has appointed dominion over the nations to His Son. One day, not only the Soviet Union, but all the Kingdoms of this world shall be shaken by His power and they shall become a part of the Kingdom of God and of His Christ.

Appendix 4 Pre-Tribulation Rapture Arguments Examined

In his book, *How Close Are We?*, Dave Hunt puts forward a number of arguments as to why the Pre-Tribulation Rapture view of the End Times is the only one which can possibly be true. These arguments are summarised as follows:

1. Jesus promised his disciples in John 14:1-3 that he was going to prepare a place for them and that he would come again and receive them to himself.
2. In Matthew 24 Jesus gives various signs that the end is near but then tells the disciples to watch and be ready because they will not know when he is coming.
3. In Daniel 9:24-27, where the 70 weeks of years for Israel are laid out (see Chapter 6 above), there is a gap between the 69th week and the 70th week. This gap commenced when Christ died and will not recommence until the rapture of the Church takes place.
4. The 'restraining influence' of 2 Thessalonians 2:7 is in fact the Church and therefore the Antichrist can only be revealed if the Church is taken out of the way. The presence of the Church is the hindrance to God's final dealings with Israel in the final seven years of history. The Church must therefore be removed in order for God's dealings with Israel to recommence.
5. Heaven is the hope and promise of the Church and therefore the Rapture must take place in order for the Church to attain to Heaven.
6. The Tribulation is the period during which the Marriage Supper of the Lamb takes place (Revelation 19:7-9) – the time when the bride is taken into the Fathers house to fulfil the type of Jewish weddings.
7. From Luke 17:26-30, it is argued that the coming of Christ will be like the days of Noah when life was continuing as normal, however, the situation we encounter in the judgements of Revelation does not present a picture of such a time but rather one in which the earth is desolated and war-ridden (Chapter 21).
8. Matthew 24:29-31 refers to a re-gathering of Israel and not the

Rapture of the Church (Chapter 21).

9. Members of the Early Church were clearly troubled that they might have missed the coming of the Lord (2 Thessalonians 1:6-10). This clearly points to the fact that they believed in a Pre-Tribulation Rapture.
10. The scriptures argue for Immanency which is taken away if we believe in anything other than a Pre-Tribulation Rapture (Chapter 23).

These arguments are laid one upon another by Mr. Hunt and would appear to point to a significant amount of evidence to support his position. The problem with them is threefold: firstly, they are built largely on inference and interpretation; secondly, they contradict or ignore those scriptures where clear teaching is given that does not fit in with the End Times scenario they ensconce; thirdly, the failure to consider any other interpretation of the scriptures cited results in a narrow minded (and at times bombastic and arrogant) view of the End Times where any who do not agree with Mr. Hunt's interpretation are labelled as 'mad' or 'ignorant'.

Let us now consider the arguments raised.

1. Jesus promise to take his disciples home

In John 14 1- 6, Jesus promises that he is going to prepare a place for the disciples (and, by inference, all subsequent followers) and will come again to take them to himself. There are a number of elements to this: firstly, Jesus is saying that his disciples have a place in Heaven with himself and that such disciples will be with him there; secondly he is promising to come again and receive his disciples to himself. This for each one of us is a blessed hope – we have a home in Heaven and Jesus will make sure we get there. Also, we have the promise of Jesus' return. Again all of us would rejoice in this, however, there is nothing in this verse which infers a specific timing for the event of Jesus' return. Mr. Hunt suggests that, in order for this to happen, there must be a period when the whole of the Church is away from the earth so that it can spend that time exclusively with Jesus in Heaven. He locates this period as being during the Tribulation, however, this is clearly an inference and not one on which we can build a doctrine. To support this, he suggests that this is the time during which the Marriage Supper of the

Lamb will take place. We will deal with this below.

Looking once more at the scripture itself, Jesus declares a number of truths here:

- In God's house there are many dwelling places;
- His return to heaven was (in part at least) to prepare a place for His disciples;
- He will return and receive them to himself, that where he is, they will also be.

From this passage we know that we have a place in heaven that Jesus himself is preparing. We also know that he will return for us and that we will always be with Him. That is as much as we can determine from these words. Inference beyond this is mere unsubstantiated speculation.

2. The 'apparent contradiction' between watching for the signs of the times and being ready for Christ's return

David Hunt argues that in Matthew 24 and 25 there is an apparent contradiction between on the one hand, Jesus giving his disciples signs to look out for to indicate that his coming is near, and on the other hand being ready because 'you do not know which day your Lord is coming'. To explain this he suggests that these two sets of statements are addressed to two different audiences: the World should look for the signs because these will take place during the Tribulation in order to confirm that Jesus Second Coming is drawing near; believers should be ready and not be looking for signs since Christ will come when they are not expecting Him. The latter audience should be looking for a secret coming and the former should be looking for a momentous, public event.

Even a cursory reading of Matthew 24 demonstrates the above position to be unsustainable (based on this passage at least). Firstly, the discourse is addressed directly to the disciples and in it Jesus is warning his disciples not to be misled or to go after any of the false messiahs who would arise. He also uses the word 'tribulation' specifically concerning what would happen to his followers during the time when 'lawlessness is increased', just before 'the end will come'. Since, this discourse is addressed to the disciples and the warnings in it are given directly to them, there is no reason for us to find a different set of people to apply them to.

Secondly, the use of the word 'elect' here is very specific. Jesus tells us that the tribulation is shortened 'for the sake of the elect'; he also says that 'false Christs and false prophets will arise…so as to mislead, if possible, even the elect'. In order to sustain the above argument we must interpret 'the elect here' as the Jews, and yet Jesus says that he has 'told his disciples in advance' so that they will not go after false Messiahs. He goes on to say that His coming will not be in secret (v.26) but will be a global event mapped out in the skies.

Thirdly, Jesus goes on, in verse 36ff, to talk about 'that day' (the one he has just described) and reminds them that, whilst they may be able to see some of the End Time events occurring, they should remain watchful because they do not know exactly when it will occur.

The suggestion that this passage can be divided between two different audiences, neither of whom is being addressed by Jesus within the discourse is poor exegesis to say the least. If one reads the whole discourse from beginning to end, it is clear that the whole passage is addressed to His disciples - the repeated use of the word 'you' makes it clear that Jesus is not looking for another set of people to whom his words should be addressed.

Concerning the point Mr. Hunt raises about there being an apparent contradiction in this passage, the truth is that this is no contradiction. On the one hand, Jesus instructs us to watch for the 'signs of the times' to know when His return is approaching; on the other hand he tells us that we do not know the exact day or hour when it will occur so we should be ready in terms of our personal walk.

3. The commencement of the seventieth week of Daniel 9

In his book, David Hunt argues that there is a gap between the cessation of the 69th week of Daniel and the commencement of the 70th week. He further argues that, since the events of this week cited in Daniel exclusively deal with Israel, the removal of the Church is the event which causes this 70th week to commence.

I have dealt with the 70 weeks of Daniel in some detail in Chapter 5 above and have no issue with Mr. Hunt's interpretation of the timing of the weeks. However, the inference that, for these weeks to commence, the Church must be removed from the world is unscriptural and unsustainable. The Bible is silent on this point.

4. The restraining influence of 2 Thessalonians 2:7 is the Church

Mr. Hunt argues that Israel's rejection of its Messiah and the formation of the Church stopped 'God's timeclock' before the 70th week of Daniel (see point 3 above). In order for this 'clock' to commence ticking again, the Church must be removed from the World since Israel will not accept their Messiah until the end of the Tribulation. Thus, it is the presence of the Church which is stopping the revelation of the Anti-Christ.

Once more, this argument is an inference with no scriptural basis. His interpretation of 2 Thessalonians 2:7 is unsustainable not only from the text but also from any other scriptures (see Chapter 3 above for a discussion on the most likely options concerning the 'restraining influence').

5. Heaven is the hope of the Church

David Hunt, in his arguments, combines John 14:2-3 with 1 Thessalonians 4:16-17 and 1 Corinthians 15:51-52 to suggest that the purpose of the rapture is to take the Church to Heaven. Whilst there is a place for believers in Heaven, neither of the latter two of these passages give any reference to Heaven. 1 Thessalonians 4 simply says that we will be 'caught up to meet him in the air and so shall we ever be with the Lord' (this is a similar point that Jesus makes in John 14:3, however he does not say that that place will be Heaven). 1 Corinthians 15: 51-52 simply says that at the last trumpet 'we shall all be changed'. Neither of these passages can be used as a justification for the Church being raptured straight to Heaven.

We can say that the Church will always be with Jesus, and since he will be coming again to reign on earth, we will return with Him to reign (see Revelation 5:10). We can also say that we will be resident in the new heavens and the new earth (Revelation 21). In addition, from John 14:2, we can say that there is a place prepared in Heaven for us to dwell in, however, we cannot say at which point in eternity that will occur.

6. The Marriage Supper of the lamb takes place during the tribulation

Scripturally, it is not clear what is meant by 'the Marriage Supper of the Lamb'. This term is only used in Revelation 19:7-10 at which point we see the bride having made herself ready and we are told that 'blessed are those who are invited to the marriage supper of the Lamb'. Further definition of what this event actually is or when it takes place is not given anywhere in scripture.

Other passages making reference to the bridegroom coming for his bride include Matthew 25:1-13, where the emphasis is on His people being ready for His coming, and Matthew 22:1-14, where Jesus' emphasis is on the invited and the uninvited guests at the wedding.

What this event actually is, cannot be determined from scripture. What we can say is that the bride is made up of 'the saints' who are clothed in fine linen which stands for 'righteous acts'. In other words, it is the coming together of Christ and His Church, once that Church has been completed in terms of its capacity and its activity.

In terms of the narrative of Revelation, this occurs directly between the fall of Babylon and the Coming of the Lord in judgement. If, as is argued by Mr Hunt, the bride is united with the bridegroom at the beginning of the Tribulation, this event is completely out of sequence in the book of Revelation. It makes no sense for an event which is supposed to have occurred at the beginning of Revelation suddenly to be mentioned near the end of Revelation.

Rather, the fact that this event is described directly in connection with the Coming of the Lord would suggest that the Marriage Supper of the Lamb occurs at, or just prior to, His coming.

7. The Days of Noah & Lot

From Luke 17:22-30 (a parallel passage to Matthew 24 -25), Mr. Hunt argues that the time of Lord's Second Coming will be a time of peace where we see life continuing in a very normal manner. In contrast with this, the judgements of the book of Revelation will create a world which is anything but in a peaceful state.

However, the emphasis Jesus gives in Luke 17 is not that the world will be at peace but that, despite pending judgement, like the inhabitants at the world prior to the flood and like the inhabitants of Sodom, there will continue to be trade and to be marriage right up until the time when that judgement falls. There is no reason to expect that it will be any different during the tribulation, despite the disruptions on earth at that time. Life has a habit of going on even in the midst of disaster.

8. The Re-gathering of Israel

Mr Hunt interprets Matthew 24:31 as a supernatural (angelically administered) re-gathering of the Jews back to the land of Israel at the time of Jesus' return.

This is a poor interpretation of this verse for a number of reasons: firstly, the use of the term 'elect' here stands in contrast with the use of the term in every other New testament Scripture, where it is always used to signify believers; secondly, nowhere else in scripture is there any indication of a supernatural re-gathering of Israel. Whilst there are many passages that refer to Jews coming back to the Land, these are already being fulfilled in our day with the re-establishment of the State of Israel and the return of Jews from all over the world in preparation for the coming of the Messiah when they will 'look up him whom they have pierced', as his feet alight on the Mount of Olives, and they accept Him as their Messiah.

Mr Hunt has interpreted this verse as the re-gathering of Israel in order to sustain his argument that this does not refer to the rapture of the Church not from any coherent exegesis. More specifically, he puts the timing of this re-gathering at the coming of the Lord which is in contradiction with the return to the land which we are currently witnessing.

I am not arguing here that there will not be a further and more widespread return to the Land of the dispersed Jews at the return of the Messiah, however, this passage does not refer to such an event.

9. The Early Church were troubled that they had missed the coming of the Lord

Mr Hunt argues that the Thessalonians were concerned that they might have missed the coming of the Lord and this proves that they believed in a Pre-Tribulation Rapture.

What is clear from 2 Thessalonians 2 is that they were actually ignorant of the End Time events and therefore Paul was trying to give them some reassurance by teaching them the truth. In this context he says that concerning 'the coming of our Lord Jesus Christ' and our gathering together unto him (the rapture), 'the Day of the Lord' will not come unless 'the man of lawlessness is revealed' first.

We know from our studies above that the Antichrist is only revealed during the Tribulation and therefore to use this very explicit and clear scripture to argue that the rapture happens prior to the Antichrist is revealed is unhelpful. Rather, Paul is arguing the exact opposite here – that the rapture only comes after the Antichrist has been revealed.

10. Immanency argues against anything but a Pre-Tribulation Rapture

Mr Hunt builds an argument that if we know that Jesus will not return until the end of the Tribulation, by watching for the signs of the times, we will know when this is going to happen (and that it cannot happen until those signs have been fulfilled). This takes away the idea that His return is immanent and will be unexpected.

This view of immanency is very narrow indeed. He uses the notion of immanency to suggest that if we can work out approximately when Jesus will return, His return will not take anyone by surprise and therefore Jesus' words concerning this will not be true. This is to overstate what Jesus actually says concerning His return. What he actually says is 'be on the alert for you do not know which day your Lord is coming'. In other words, the emphasis is on us being ready because we won't know the day on which it will occur.

Jesus intention here is to ensure we are not sleeping when he returns (as confirmed in the first two parables in Matthew 25). Because we can read some of the signs of the times, we could become complacent and this is what Jesus warns us against in these parables.

Appendix 5 Miscellaneous Footnotes

Foot Note 14

Accounts indicate that the garden was built by King Nebuchadnezzar, who ruled the city for 43 years starting in 605 BC (There is a less-reliable, alternative story that the gardens were built by the Assyrian Queen Semiramis during her five year reign starting in 810 BC). This was the height of the city's power and influence and King Nebuchadnezzar constructed an astonishing array of temples, streets, palaces and walls.

According to these accounts, the gardens were built to cheer up Nebuchadnezzar's homesick wife, Amyitis. Amyitis, daughter of the king of the Medes, was married to Nebuchadnezzar to create an alliance between the nations. The land she came from, though, was green, rugged and mountainous, and she found the flat, sun-baked terrain of Mesopotamia depressing. The king decided to recreate her homeland by building an artificial mountain with rooftop gardens.

The Hanging Gardens probably did not really "hang" in the sense of being suspended from cables or ropes. The name comes from an inexact translation of the Greek word kremastos or the Latin word pensilis, which mean not just "hanging", but "overhanging" as in the case of a terrace or balcony.

The Greek geographer Strabo, who described the gardens in first century BC, wrote, "It consists of vaulted terraces raised one above another, and resting upon cube-shaped pillars. These are hollow and filled with earth to allow trees of the largest sizes to be planted. The pillars, the vaults, and terraces are constructed of baked brick and asphalt."

"The ascent to the highest story is by stairs, and at their side are water engines, by means of which persons, appointed expressly for the purpose, are continually employed in raising water from the Euphrates into the garden."

Strabo touches on what, to the ancients, was probably the most amazing part of the garden. Babylon rarely received rain and for the garden to survive it would have had to have been irrigated by using water from the nearby Euphrates River. That meant lifting the water far into the air so it could flow down through the terraces, watering the plants at each level. This was probably done by means of a "chain pump."

A chain pump is two large wheels, one above the other, connected by a chain. On the chain are hung buckets. Below the bottom wheel is a pool with the water source. As the wheel is turned, the buckets dip into the pool and pick up water. The chain then lifts them to the upper wheel, where the buckets are tipped and dumped into an upper pool. The chain then carries the empty ones back down to be refilled.

The pool at the top of the gardens could then be released by gates into channels which acted as artificial streams to water the gardens. The pump wheel below was attached to a shaft and a handle. By turning the handle, slaves provided the power to run the contraption.

Construction of the garden wasn't only complicated by getting the water up to the top, but also by having to avoid allowing the liquid to ruin the foundation once it was released. Since stone was difficult to get on the Mesopotamian plain, most of the architecture in Babel utilized brick. The bricks were composed of clay mixed with chopped straw and baked in the sun. The bricks were then joined with bitumen, a slimy substance, which acted as a mortar. These bricks quickly dissolved when soaked with water. For most buildings in Babel this wasn't a problem because rain was so rare. However, the gardens were continually exposed to irrigation and the foundation had to be protected.

Diodorus Siculus, a Greek historian, stated that the platforms on which the garden stood consisted of huge slabs of stone (otherwise unheard of in Babel), covered with layers of reed, asphalt and tiles. Over this was put "a covering with sheets of lead, that the water which drenched through the earth might not rot the foundation. Upon all these was laid earth of a convenient depth, sufficient for the growth of the greatest trees. When the soil was laid even and smooth, it was planted with all sorts of trees, which both for greatness and beauty might delight the spectators."

How big were the gardens? Diodorus tells us it was about 400 feet wide by 400 feet long and more than 80 feet high. Other accounts indicate the height was equal to the outer city walls. Walls that Herodotus said were 320 feet high.

In any case the gardens were an amazing sight: a green, leafy, artificial mountain rising off the plain. But did it actually exist? After all, Herodotus never mentions it.

This was one of the questions that occurred to German archaeologist Robert Koldewey in 1899. For centuries before that the ancient city of Babel was nothing but a mound of muddy debris. Though unlike many ancient locations, the city's position was well-known, nothing visible remained of its architecture. Koldewey dug on the Babel site for some fourteen years and unearthed many of its features including the outer walls, inner walls, foundation of the Tower of Babel, Nebuchadnezzar's palaces and the wide processional roadway which passed through the heart of the city.

While excavating the Southern Citadel, Koldewey discovered a basement with fourteen large rooms with stone arch ceilings. Ancient records indicated that only two locations in the city had made use of stone, the north wall of the Northern Citadel, and the Hanging Gardens. The north wall of the Northern Citadel had already been found and had, indeed, contained stone. This made it seem likely that Koldewey had found the cellar of the gardens.

He continued exploring the area and discovered many of the features reported by Diodorus. Finally a room was unearthed with three large, strange holes in the floor. Koldewey concluded this had been the location of the chain pumps that raised the water to the garden's roof.

The foundations that Koldewey discovered measured some 100 by 150 feet. Smaller than the measurements described by ancient historians, but still impressive.

While Koldewey was convinced he'd found the gardens, some modern archaeologists call his discovery into question arguing that this location is too far from the river to have be irrigated with the amount of water that would have been required. Also tablets recently found at the site suggest that the location was used for administrative and/or storage purposes, not as a pleasure garden.

Wherever the location of the gardens were, we can only wonder if Queen Amyitis was happy with her fantastic present, or if she continued to pine for the green mountains of her homeland.

Foot Note 15

The Babylonians had taken the field and were awaiting his (Cyrus') approach. When he arrived near the city they attacked him, but were defeated and forced to retire inside their defences; they already knew of Cyrus' restless ambition and had watched his successive acts of aggression against one nation after another, and as they had taken the precaution of accumulating in Babylon a stock of provisions sufficient to last many years, they were able to regard the prospect of a siege with indifference. The siege dragged on, no progress was made, and Cyrus was beginning to despair of success. Then somebody suggested or he himself thought up the plan: he stationed part of his force at the point where the Euphrates flows into the city and another contingent at the opposite end where it flows out. He gave orders to both groups to force an entrance along the riverbed as soon as they saw the water was shallow enough. Then, taking with him all his non-combatant troops, he withdrew to the spot where Nitocris [Belshazzar's mother] had excavated the lake, and proceeded to repeat the operation which the queen had previously performed: by means of a cutting he diverted the water into the lake (which was then a marsh) and in this way greatly reduced the depth of water in the actual bed of the river that it became fordable, and the Persian army, which had been left at Babylon for the purpose, entered the river. Now only deep enough to reach about the middle of a man's thigh, and making their way along it, got into the town. If the Babylonians had learnt what Cyrus was doing or had seen it for themselves in time, they could have let the Persians enter and then, by shutting the gates which led to the waterside and manning the walls on either side of the river, they could have caught them in a trap and wiped them out. But, as it was, they were taken by surprise. The Babylonians themselves say that owing to the great size of the city the outskirts were captured without the people in the centre knowing anything about it; there was a festival going on, and they continued to dance and enjoy themselves, until they learned the news the hard way. That then is the story of the first capture of Babylon.

Bibliography

Bright, J. Jeremiah 1965 Anchor Bible, Doubleday

Berkhof, Louis Systematic Theology 1984 The Banner of Truth Trust ISBN 0 85151 056 6

Clarke, Adam Commentary and Critical Notes in Six Volumes Ward, Lock & Co.

Collins, Owen The Definitive Bible Commentary 1999 Owen Collins ISBN 0 551 03175 1

Grudem, Wayne Systematic Theology 1994 Inter-varsity Press ISBN 0 85110 652 8

Guthrie, Donald New Testament Theology 1981 Inter-varsity Press ISBN 0 85111 742 2

Herodotus, The Histories Penguin Books Revised edition 1996, Translated by Aubrey De Selincourt, Revised with introductory notes by John Marincola

Hunt, Dave How Close Are We? 1993 Harvest House Publishers ISBN 1-89081-904-1

Jopsephus, The Essential Writings 1988 translated and edited by Paul L. Maier ISBN 0 8254 2963 3

Kidner, Derek The Message of Jeremiah 2003 Inter-varsity Press ISBN 0 85110 779 6

Matthew, David Church Adrift 1989 Marshall Paperbacks ISBN 0 551 01275 7

Prince, Derek Foundations for Righteous Living Derek Prince Ministries - UK ISBN 1 901144 05 4

Spurgeon, Charles The Second Coming of Christ 1996 Whitaker House ISBN 0 88368 380 6

Stott, John What Christ thinks of the Church 1990 Angus Hudson Ltd. ISBN 1 899788 42 5

Unger, Merrill F.Unger's Bible Dictionary 1983 Paperback Edition Moody Press ISBN 0 8024 0418 9

Webb, Barry The Message of Isaiah 2003 Inter-varsity Press ISBN 0

85111 167 X

Webb, Barry The Message of Zechariah 2003 Inter-varsity Press ISBN 0 85111 294 3

Wood, Michael, In the Footsteps of Alexander The Great 1997,2001 BBC Worldwide Limited

ISBN 0 563 53783 3

Web Sites

http://www.forerunner.com/forerunner/X0664_Gog_and_Magog.htm Jay Rogers